Sectoral Clash and Industrialization
in Latin America

by

Dale Story

Foreign and Comparative Studies/Latin American Series, No. 2

Maxwell School of Citizenship and Public Affairs

Syracuse University

1981

Library of Congress Cataloging in Publication Data

Story, Dale, 1950-
    Sectoral clash and industrialization in Latin
America.

    (Foreign and comparative studies : Latin American
series ; no. 2)
    Bibliography: p.
    1. Industry and state--Latin America. 2. Latin
America--Industries. I. Title. II. Series: Foreign
and comparative studies : Latin American series ; 2.
HD3616.L32S75   338.98   80-28553
ISBN 0-915984-93-8

CONTENTS

iv

LIST OF FIGURES

LIST OF TABLES

Chapter 1

INTRODUCTION*

One of the most important issues in the process of industrialization in Latin American countries concerns the degree to which a
clash occurs between the emerging industrial sector and the primary
product export sector, either mineral or agricultural. The timing
of this clash, its intensity, and the relative role of various economic actors in initiating it have a significant impact on economic
and political development. Factors that are affected by the pattern
of sectoral clash include economic growth, the timing of industrialization, the degree of class conflict, and the formation of political coalitions.

In a narrow sense, sectoral clash can be defined as conflict
among economic sectors over the allocation and transfer of resources.
More broadly, this clash stems from conflicting political ideologies,
social attitudes, and economic interests among economic sectors.
Especially in the Latin American context, this often involves public
economic policies that extract resources from one sector and allocate them to another. The focus here is on industrialization policies in the period of transition from export-led growth to inward-
oriented industrialization. Sectoral clash may also involve the
differentiation of interests, such as the formation of separate interest associations for industrialists and their increasing attempts
to influence policy decisions that are adverse to other sectors.

The importance of sectoral clash in various historical settings
has been recognized for some time. For example, Karl Marx and
Friedrich Engels (1955:19-20), in their analysis of the history of
the class struggle, stress the importance of the struggle of the

*I would like to acknowledge the helpful comments of David
Collier, John Gillespie, Paul Kuznets, and Richard Stryker. This
research was supported in part by a grant from the Organized Research Fund of the University of Texas at Arlington.

industrial bourgeoisie with the aristocracy. In another setting
Barrington Moore (1966:111-55) emphasizes sectoral conflict between
the cotton-growing South, the free-farming West, and the rapidly in-
dustrializing North as factors leading to the American Civil War.
He argues that the manner in which this sectoral clash was resolved
has played a crucial role in shaping subsequent patterns of political
change in the United States. A.F.K. Organski (1965:10, 56-156) argues that sectoral clash is a major factor in the industrial stage
of political development. Finally, with reference to Latin America,
Markos Mamalakis (1969a and 1971a) posits a theory of sectoral clash
that describes the sectoral influences on the transition from a "traditional, government-export sector coalition" to a "modern, government-industry coalition."[1] The perspective developed by Mamalakis
has been applied by various authors to studies of Argentina, Chile,
Cuba, and Mexico.[2]

This monograph compares patterns of sectoral clash in five Latin
American countries: Argentina, Brazil, Chile, Mexico, and Venezuela.
These countries are among the most advanced countries in Latin America, and they represent a wide range of experiences in terms of the
emergence of the industrial sector and its conflict with the traditional export sector.

In comparing patterns of sectoral clash in Latin America, three
crucial issues are addressed: (1) who initiates the clash; (2) the
timing of the clash; and (3) the effect of this clash on industrialization policies, on industrial growth, and on political change.
Chapter 2 discusses the question of who initiates the clash: whether
sectoral clash is primarily initiated by autonomous economic actors
making demands on either the state or other economic actors, or
whether it is primarily initiated from within the state (by the
ruling party or by the military, for example) through the imposi-
tion on private economic actors of policies which effectively reallocate resources. Chapter 3 relates these distinctions to issues
regarding industrialization policies: the timing of sectoral clash
in relation to the period in which industrialization policies are
emphasized; and the degree of emphasis that these industrialization
policies place on achieving diversified and integrated industrial

growth. Finally, the Conclusion (Chapter 4) discusses the impact
of sectoral clash on the relative success of industrial progress
and on political change in the five countries.

Patterns of Sectoral Clash

The distinction in terms of who initiates the sectoral clash
is not intended to be a strict dichotomy between autonomously initiated and state-initiated clash, but rather these types are only
polar ends of a spectrum along which cases can be arrayed. In
cases of autonomously initiated clash, political and economic conflict among sectors occurs largely independent of the state. On
the other hand, state-initiated clash is largely due to governmental actions which reallocate resources among economic sectors.

In the comparison of cases, one might expect to find recurring
patterns in the relationships among who initiates sectoral clash,
the timing of the clash, and the emphasis of industrialization policies. Sectoral clash initiated by the state might be more likely
to occur later than autonomously initiated clash, to coincide with
the most significant phase of industrial promotion policies, and
to produce policies that do not emphasize industrial integration.
This is probable for several reasons. First, because the industrial sector will not have taken the initiative in sectoral clash,
state-initiated clash might be a "delayed" attempt to reallocate
resources among economic sectors. Second, industrialization policies might be an integral component of a state strategy of sectoral
discrimination. In such cases, the industrial sector will not have
challenged the dominance of the export sector; hence, the state
will assume the role of encouraging industry, and industrial promotion policies could become significant aspects of sectoral clash.
Third, state-initiated sectoral clash might be less likely to produce effective industrialization policies that emphasize diversified growth, because the state has to assume the role of artificially encouraging the dominance of industry. Consequently, there
could be a greater chance for severe discrimination against certain sectors and for the misallocation of resources.

Sectoral clash initiated primarily by national industrialists independent of the state might be more likely to appear earlier than state-initiated clash, to precede the crucial phase of industrialization policies, and to produce policies that stress industrial integration. Several reasons for this pattern can be suggested. The role of the state in these cases in establishing industry as an equal or even a dominant partner in relation to other sectors should be less important, so sectoral clash could be less likely to coincide with industrialization policies. In particular, this type of sectoral clash might occur relatively early, since private economic actors are taking the initiative in challenging the export elite. In addition, the industrialization policies might be more likely to allocate resources in an equitable fashion and to emphasize diversified growth, since they will not be a part of a state program to reallocate resources among sectors.

Notes

[1] Also see O'Donnell (1973:57-58).

[2] Mamalakis (1965), Barraza (1969), Merkx (1969), and Domínguez (1971).

Chapter 2

WHO INITIATES SECTORAL CLASH

One finds considerable variation among cases in the degree to
which the clash is autonomously initiated or state-initiated. In
Argentina, sectoral clash occurred between 1946 and 1955, when President Juan Perón redistributed resources from the agricultural sector
to the urban sector. Sectoral clash in Brazil began in the 1920s
as important industrialists in São Paulo, the industrial heartland
of Brazil, began to challenge the economic and political power of
the agricultural sector, particularly the coffee-growing elites.
In Chile, sectoral clash took place as income from the foreign-
owned copper companies was distributed among domestic sectors by
the state. Sectoral clash in Mexico was one aspect of the multi-
faceted Mexican Revolution that pitted peasants, industrial labor,
and certain domestic entrepreneurial groups against the foreign-
dominated export elite. Finally, in Venezuela sectoral clash took
the form of the state-enforced redistribution of income from the
foreign-owned petroleum sector into domestic sectors.

These are, of course, not the only instances of sectoral clash
in each of these countries. Conflicts among economic sectors have
occurred in other time periods and under different circumstances.
The focus in this study is on the most important episodes of sectoral clash between the industrial sector and the primary products
export sector. These episodes also tend to be the earliest instances of a clash between industry and the export sector. The
assumption is that these early sectoral clashes influenced not
only subsequent outbreaks of sectoral clash but also subsequent
patterns of economic and political change.

The empirical research that has been done on sectoral clash
in Latin America has involved a few isolated case studies that
allow few opportunities for comparison. Therefore, the major tasks

5

of this study in terms of comparing patterns of sectoral clash are
to collect the necessary information and data on sectoral clash in
each country and to narratively present the details that substan-
tiate the major comparisons among countries.

Four economic indicators will be used to show the effect of
sectoral clash. The first two, internal terms of trade and relative productivity, are presented across time for each country in
the tables at the end of this chapter. Trends in domestic terms
of trade should reflect relative changes between sectors in levels
of demand, efficiency, or economic resources, while relative productivity should indicate a sector's capacity to generate a resource
surplus.[1] The other two economic indicators are income transfers
among sectors and comparisons of public and private investment rates
in sectors. These data have proven very difficult to collect for
all nations, so they have been selectively reported for the countries and the time periods for which they are available.

Argentina

Argentina is a case of intense state-initiated sectoral clash.
Sectoral clash in Argentina was not evident until the Perón period
(1946-55), which saw the appearance of public policies aimed at
extracting resources from the agrarian sector. This is the most
extreme instance of state-initiated sectoral clash considered in
this study, as public policies were the primary instrument in the
conflict between agriculture and industry. These policies were not
so much a response to demands on the state made by influential industrial interests as they were aspects of a state strategy aimed
at pleasing the two most important coalition members: the military
and urban labor.

The first genuine threat to Argentina's dominant agro-export
sector came with the Depression in 1930, when the rural sector was
hurt by three new developments: (1) deteriorating external terms
of trade; (2) stagnation of external demand; and (3) growth of domestic demand for agricultural products at a rate lower than the
growth rate of the economy as a whole.[2] The value of total exports
declined relative to the value of industrial production over the
next twenty-five years, and the growth rate of the rural sector,

which from 1900 to 1930 averaged 3.5 percent annually, shrank to
slightly over 1 percent annually (Díaz Alejandro, 1970:67-79). The
agro-export sector was no longer completely dominant, but at the
same time clash between agriculture and industry was minimal. In-
stead, these two sectors, especially at the elite level, became
allied under the restored political hegemony of the Conservative
party.[3]

From 1932 to 1938 the government of Augustin P. Justo tended
to favor the interests of the export elites (Freels, 1968:18; and
Goldwert, 1974:48-49). The Roca-Runciman Treaty of 1933 with Great
Britain exchanged a British commitment not to reduce its purchases
of Argentine chilled beef below the level of that in 1932 for much
more important concessions by the Argentine government.[4] Argentina
promised to allow foreign control of 85 percent of its meat expor-
ting business, "benevolent treatment" for British capital in Argentina, the use of Argentina's sterling balance for the service of
the debt to Great Britain, a reduction of tariffs on British goods
to 1930 levels, and the return of British coal to the free import
duties list (Whitaker, 1964:92-93). Furthermore, a grain regula-
ting board was created in November of 1933 to insure higher prices
for Argentine grain growers. This board purchased grain at fixed
prices about 20 percent above market prices and sold the grain to
exporters at competitive world prices. The difference was covered
by profits from the Exchange Control Commission (Phelps, 1938:71).
All of these policies were designed to benefit the agro-export
sector.

Data on internal terms of trade and relative productivity
reflect the continued dominance of the agro-export sector at least
up to the latter years of the 1930s and indicate a lack of sectoral
clash between the growing industrial sector and the entrenched
cattle-raising and grain-growing export oligarchy (see Tables 2.1
and 2.2). After several years in the late twenties and early thir-
ties of turning in favor of industry, the domestic terms of trade
from 1932 to 1937 shifted toward the agricultural sector. Major
shifts in favor of industry occurred from 1930 to 1932. Then the
downward slope favoring agriculture from 1932 to 1937 coincided

Table 2.1
Relative Productivity--Argentina
(Percent of GNP / Percent of Labor Force)

	A Labor Force (%)	B GNP (%)	C A / B
1925			
Agriculture	31.6	25.3	0.80
Manufacturing	20.6	18.4	0.89
Other	47.8	56.3	1.18
1930			
Agriculture	30.8	23.1	0.75
Manufacturing	20.6	18.6	0.90
Other	48.6	58.3	1.20
1935			
Agriculture	31.0	28.4	0.92
Manufacturing	20.8	19.3	0.93
Other	48.3	52.3	1.08
1940			
Agriculture	29.6	26.3	0.89
Manufacturing	22.7	27.9	1.23
Other	47.8	45.8	0.96
1945			
Agriculture	27.3	23.7	0.87
Manufacturing	24.2	30.4	1.26
Other	48.5	45.9	0.95
1950			
Agriculture	24.4	19.6	0.80
Manufacturing	23.0	29.4	1.28
Other	52.6	51.0	0.97
1955			
Agriculture	23.0	20.0	0.87
Manufacturing	21.6	29.2	1.35
Other	55.5	50.8	0.91
1960			
Agriculture	19.8	17.7	0.89
Manufacturing	25.2	31.3	1.23
Other	44.9	51.1	1.14
1970			
Agriculture	15.3	15.3	1.00
Manufacturing	19.7	35.6	1.81
Other	56.3	49.2	0.87

NOTE: Agriculture includes livestock, fishing, and mining. Other includes construction; electricity, gas, and water; commerce, transportation, and communications; and all services.

SOURCES: Labor data for 1925-55 are from United Nations Economic Commission for Latin America, The Process of Industrial Development in Latin America, Statistical Annex, 1966, p. 13. All other labor data are from International Labor Office, International Yearbook of Labor Statistics. GNP data for 1925-35 are from Díaz Alejandro (1970: 420). All other GNP are from United Nations Economic Commission for Latin America, Statistical Bulletin for Latin America 1972.

Table 2.2

Internal Terms of Trade--Argentina
(Industrial Prices / Agricultural Prices)
1960 = 1.00

Year	Value
1926:	0.76
1927:	0.75
1928:	0.65
1929:	0.70
1930:	0.83
1931:	1.11
1932:	1.26
1933:	1.24
1934:	1.13
1935:	1.09
1936:	1.01
1937:	0.82
1938:	0.92
1939:	1.08
1940:	1.12
1941:	1.28
1942:	1.43
1943:	1.38
1944:	1.55
1945:	1.30
1946:	1.08
1947:	1.27
1948:	1.31
1949:	1.46
1950:	1.33
1951:	1.19
1952:	1.12
1953:	1.06
1954:	1.13
1955:	1.23
1956:	1.09
1957:	0.99
1958:	1.07
1959:	0.89
1960:	1.00
1961:	1.13
1962:	1.10
1963:	0.99
1964:	0.83
1965:	1.02
1966:	1.07
1967:	1.08
1968:	1.06
1969:	0.97

.60 .70 .80 .90 1.00 1.10 1.20 1.30 1.40 1.50 1.60 1.70 1.80

Note:
   The price index for industrial goods is taken from: (1926-34), wholesale
price index for nonrural goods; and (1935-69), implicit GDP deflator for manufacturing. Price index for agricultural goods is taken from: (1926-34), wholesale price index for rural goods; and (1935-69), implicit GDP deflator for agriculture.

Sources:
   1926-34:   Díaz Alejandro, 1970, p. 458.
   1935-50:   Díaz Alejandro, 1970, p. 454.
   1951-64:   Díaz Alejandro, 1980, p. 455.
   1965-69:   Banco Central de La Republica Argentina, Boletín Estadístico.

with the conservative, agrarian-oriented Justo regime. Relative productivity of the agricultural sector improved from 1930 to 1935, and then diminished only slightly by 1940. In terms of both labor and income, agriculture played a larger role in the economy than industry until 1940, when industry's share of the GNP passed that of agriculture.

The most intense period of sectoral clash was from 1946 to 1955, as the state initiated policies that discriminated against the agrarian sector. There had been a few earlier instances of sectoral cleavage in which the state was not the primary instigator: a demonstration by organized industrial interests against the Roca-Runciman Treaty in 1933 (see note 4 here) and organized opposition from agrarian interest associations to Finance Minister Pinedo's Plan of Economic Reactiviation in 1940.[5] But the interests of industry and agriculture were not pitted continuously against one another until Perón began to redistribute income from the rural to the urban sector. The chief policy instrument for this redistribution was the Argentine Trade Promotion Institute (Instituto Argentino de Promoción del Intercambio, or IAPI).

The IAPI was created by Decree No. 15350 of May 1946 with its stated purpose being "to promote the development of foreign and domestic commerce and to undertake activities designed to foster those purposes" (Salaberren, et al., 1951:167). It was given broad powers to buy or sell various kinds of property and products, and under Perón's first Five-Year Plan (1947-51) the IAPI purchased agricultural products at low prices and sold them at the highest possible prices to European nations (Scobie, 1971:234; and Fillol, 1961:52). The profits accrued to the state rather than to the agrarian producers, and the state distributed them within the urban sector. Another instrument used to diminish agricultural profits was the continued overvaluing of the peso which became especially high from 1946 to 1955 (Ferrer, 1967:169-74; and Kenworthy, 1973: 42).

Data on income distribution and wage levels clearly show the impact of the discrimination against the agricultural sector (Silverman, 1968-69). From 1943 to 1949 urban labor's share of

national income rose from about 45 percent to 59 percent with most
of this increase coming in only two years from 1947 to 1949. An
index of nonlabor income shows the income of landlords ("rentiers")
dropping from a base of 100 in 1943 to 34.7 in 1952. As with the
increase in urban labor's income, the largest drop in landowners'
income was concentrated in the years 1946-49. As final evidence
of the direction of income redistribution in the second half of
the 1940s, from 1944 to 1949 industrial wages rose substantially
faster than agricultural wages.

Though these policies did lead to a major extraction of resources from agriculture, industrial dominance was never achieved.
For example, the reallocation of resources did not benefit industrial entrepreneurs as much as industrial labor and those in the
services sector. In Silverman's data, the managerial index of
income moved upward at the same rate as the index for industrial
workers until 1948, when decreases in managerial income began to
be much greater than those in industrial workers' income. Also,
Díaz Alejandro (1971:228-43) says that the flow of factors out of
agriculture during the Peronist period did not go so much into the
import-substituting manufacturing sector as into the services sector.

The lack of industrial dominance is also evident in the most
recent policies of Economic Minister Martínez de Hoz.[6] Through
his policies in 1976 and 1977 that have weakened the domestic market, decreased demand, and restricted industrial credit, Martínez
de Hoz has reversed the sectoral discrimination that Perón instituted. Now the land-owning oligarchy is being favored, while domestic industry is being attacked as unproductive.

Brazil

Sectoral clash in Brazil was primarily initiated by the economic elites rather than by the state. The major period of sectoral clash in Brazil was from 1920 to 1940, and the principal
manifestations occurred within the private sphere and were independent of state interference. Brazilian sectoral clash stemmed
from attempts by private industrial entrepreneurs, especially

those in São Paulo, to influence state policy and to challenge the traditional export elite. However, one feature of postwar economic policy in Brazil does suggest an important state role in sectoral clash: the major extraction of resources from the export sector between 1945 and 1961 similar to that in Argentina in the late 1940s.

There were various important ties between the coffee-dominated export sector and the emerging industrial sector during the latter part of the nineteenth century and the first two decades of the twentieth century, but these ties began to unravel in the 1920s. In fact, as early as 1880 a group of industrialists, dissatisfied with their inability to raise tariffs through their membership in the Commercial Association of Rio de Janeiro, broke off to form the first interest group exclusively for industrialists, the Industrial Association (Schmitter, 1971:145-46). This Association was short-lived, however, and it was not until after the turn of the century that industrialists, especially in the state of São Paulo, began to evolve into a distinct group with interests separate from those of the coffee planters and the merchants.[7] In the 1920s, Paulista manufacturers became especially dissatisfied with their organizational ties to commercial interests, and in 1928 they challenged the domination of merchants in the Commercial Association of São Paulo with a dissident slate of candidates for the directorate. The industrial slate lost, but shortly thereafter the industrialists formed a separate organization, the Center of Industries of the State of São Paulo (Centro das Indústrias do Estado de São Paulo, or CIESP).[8] The CIESP, led by immigrant entrepreneurs Francisco Matarazzo and Roberto Simonsen, soon became the most important spokesman for industrial interests.

It is evident that the ideology expressed by the CIESP placed Brazilian industry in conflict with other sectors. In his inaugural address as vice-president of the CIESP, Simonsen argued that Brazil had to pursue industrial growth to maintain independence. In reply, the Commercial Association of Rio de Janeiro charged Simonsen with trying to alienate commercial interests, and the Brazilian Rural Society attacked his speech as "ultra-protectionist." Matarazzo

and Simonsen tried to smooth over differences with other sectors.
"Nonetheless, and in spite of this superficial public harmony, the
founding of the CIESP in 1928 marks the moment at which these [sec-
toral] interests took separate courses once and for all" (Schmitter,
1971:148).

Sectoral differences intensified in the early 1930s during the
early Vargas period when economic policies were still oriented toward the coffee-growing elite.[9] Only weeks after the 1930 Revolution, Simonsen was jailed and not released until a general amnesty
was granted. He emerged blaming the coffee planters for sacrificing
the interests of other productive sectors and alluding to the "class
struggle" between planters and industrialists (Dean, 1969:184-85).
The pre-Estado Novo policies of Vargas favoring free trade and the
coffee interests continued to elicit hostility from the industrialists, who resented a 1931 act putting their associations under federal control, the 1935 and 1936 trade agreements that relaxed some
tariffs, and other measures they interpreted as favoring the agrarian sector and the working class.[10]

In addition to political differences, industrialists began to
separate themselves economically from the agro-export sector between
1920 and 1940. Industrial entrepreneurs not linked to the export
economy began to prosper. Also, investment in manufacturing by the
coffee elite and the importers became less important than that by
the industrial entrepreneurs themselves (Dean, 1969:113, 126). In
this manner, industry was no longer as dependent upon the export
sector as before 1920, and by 1940 industry had replaced agriculture as the dominant sector (Leff, 1968:28). Although data are not
available before the Second World War, Table 2.3 shows that in 1944
industrial prices were at their highest level vis-à-vis agricultural
prices for the entire period from 1944 to 1973. Also, productivity
data indicate that the Brazilian industrial sector was fairly efficient and modernized in 1940, since only Mexico had higher relative
productivity in industry (see Tables 2.4 and 2.5).

The one feature of postwar economic policy in Brazil that reflected a state role in sectoral clash was the extreme discrimination against the export sector in the government's foreign exchange

Table 2.3

Internal Terms of Trade--Brazil
(Industrial Prices / Agricultural Prices)
1952 = 1.00

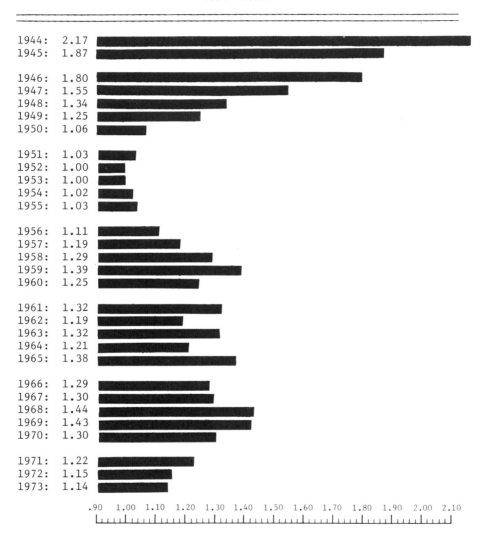

1944:	2.17
1945:	1.87
1946:	1.80
1947:	1.55
1948:	1.34
1949:	1.25
1950:	1.06
1951:	1.03
1952:	1.00
1953:	1.00
1954:	1.02
1955:	1.03
1956:	1.11
1957:	1.19
1958:	1.29
1959:	1.39
1960:	1.25
1961:	1.32
1962:	1.19
1963:	1.32
1964:	1.21
1965:	1.38
1966:	1.29
1967:	1.30
1968:	1.44
1969:	1.43
1970:	1.30
1971:	1.22
1972:	1.15
1973:	1.14

.90 1.00 1.10 1.20 1.30 1.40 1.50 1.60 1.70 1.80 1.90 2.00 2.10

Sources:
    1944-68: Fundacão Getúlio Vargas, Conjuntura Economica, October
              1969, pp. 98-99.
    1969-73: Fundacão Getúlio Vargas, Conjuntura Economica, December
              1973, pp. 89-98.

Table 2.4

Relative Productivity--Brazil
(Percent of GNP / Percent of Labor Force)

	A Labor Force (%)	B GNP (%)	C A / B
1940			
Agriculture	67.4	25.8	0.38
Industry	12.8	19.5	1.52
Services	19.8	54.6	2.76
1950			
Agriculture	57.8	26.6	0.46
Industry	15.8	23.5	1.49
Services	26.1	49.8	1.91
1960			
Agriculture	51.6	22.5	0.44
Industry	24.8	25.2	1.02
Services	23.6	52.3	2.22
1970			
Agriculture	44.2	17.1	0.39
Industry	17.8	29.5	1.66
Services	32.9	53.4	1.62

NOTE: Agriculture includes livestock and fishing. Industry includes mining, manufacturing, construction, electricity, gas, and water. Services includes commerce, transportation, and communications.

GNP data given for 1940 are actually for 1939. That for 1970 are actually for 1969.

SOURCES: All labor force data are from International Labor Office, International Yearbook of Labor Statistics. All GNP data are from United Nations Economic Commission for Latin America, Statistical Bulletin for Latin America 1972.

Table 2.5

Relative Productivity in Industry*

Mexico (1940)	Brazil (1940)	Argentina (1940)	Venezuela (1950)	Chile (1940)
1.86	1.52	1.23	1.02	0.96

Sources: Tables 2.1, 2.4, 2.9, 2.11, 2.13.

*These data across countries are not <u>exactly</u> comparable because the original sources do not always aggregate sectors in the same manner. The notes below each table explain the aggregations. Construction, electricity, gas, and water in all five countries employ only a small share of the labor force and produce only a small amount of the national product. For the three countries in which mining is a significant sector--Chile, Mexico, and Venezuela--relative productivity has been calculated separately for this sector. So, the differences in aggregation should have little effect in comparing relative productivities across countries.

policy. This bias against exports took the form of an overvalued exchange rate which lasted from roughly 1945 to 1961.[11] From 1945 to 1953 the exchange rate was maintained at 18.50 cruzeiros per dollar, which became more overvalued each year as inflation soared. In 1953 the multiple exchange system only perpetuated the overvalued rate for exports, and it was not until 1959 that exports were being transferred to the free rate. By 1961 all exports, except for coffee, were allocated exchange at the free rate.

The rationale for the overvalued exchange rate was to keep coffee prices high and to maximize the government's export earnings of foreign exchange. But this rate priced non-coffee exports out of the world market by making them too expensive, and these exports declined some 4 percent from 1947/49 to 1960/62. The rate was also an implicit export tax on coffee producers who had to convert their dollar earnings at an exchange rate much lower than the rates used by importers. This was a subsidy for the importing of machinery and raw materials needed by the industrial sector, while manufactured imports that would compete with local products were restricted by protectionist measures. The implicit tax on coffee, as well as the fact that after 1950 coffee prices rose more slowly than industrial prices or other agricultural prices, held the increase in coffee exports between

1947:49 and 1960:62 to only 34 percent (about 2.6 percent annually.)

The overvaluation obviously contributed to sectoral cleavage, since it reduced the income of the export sector and served as a subsidy for certain industrial inputs. It was primarily a policy initiated by state administrators whose purpose was to alleviate balance of payments problems by increasing the government's foreign exchange receipts. There is no evidence that industrialists favored this policy, especially since its long-term effect was to hamper industrial growth due to import shortages. Therefore, though the major period of sectoral clash in which industry emerged as the dominant sector was initiated by industrialists in the 1920s, sectoral clash in the form of discrimination against exports was perpetuated in the postwar period by a state-initiated policy.

Chile

Sectoral clash in Chile was state-initiated, but Chile's variant of state-initiated sectoral clash differs from Argentina chiefly in the type of export sector involved. The Argentine export sector has been somewhat diversified in terms of the type of products and the geographic location, whereas the Chilean export sector has been dominated by one mineral product—copper—and has been located in a geographic enclave (Cardoso and Faletto, 1973:48-53). Also, the Argentine export sector has been domestically owned, while the Chilean copper extract industry was almost wholly foreign-controlled until 1971.

The state-initiated effort to extract resources from the export sector and to subsidize industry began with the economic policies initiated in 1931-32, especially exchange control and multiple exchange rates (Mamalakis, 1965:54-59; and Reynolds, 1965:233). The mineral producers were the first ones required to sell their foreign exchange earnings to the Central Bank at the grossly overvalued official rate. This amounted to an implicit tax on mineral products in that the mining companies had to buy local currency for local expenses at the fixed rate of 19.37 pesos/dollar while the free rate was rising much higher. At the same time, the industrial sector benefited from the subsidy that the overvalued exchange rate provided for the imported inputs necessary for manufacturing growth.

These policies were the beginning of a long-term sectoral clash in which the state gradually attempted to assert its influence over the foreign-dominated export sector and to reap more of the profits from the extraction of this natural resource.[12] The rationale for the foreign exchange policies toward the copper companies in the early 1930s was that the government's share of copper receipts fell from $33 million in 1929 to $8 million in 1933. "The government reacted against this setback in export earnings by increasing the taxation of the Gran Minería [the foreign copper companies], and by imposing an artificially high rate of exchange on the companies" (Reynolds, 1965:233).

It was not until 1939, however, that the government began to subsidize industry directly through the resources extracted from the copper producers, as opposed to the period from 1931 to 1938 when this transfer of resources was done indirectly through the differential effect on the two sectors of exchange control. In 1939 the Chilean Development Corporation (Corporación de Fomento de la Producción, or CORFO) was created, ostensibly to aid in the earth-quake recovery effort but more specifically to direct investments toward areas, especially infrastructural projects, linked to import substitution (Mamalakis, 1969b). This attempt to aid industrialization directly affected the export sector since the establishment of CORFO was financed by an additional 15 percent tax on the copper companies. Thus, the creation of CORFO brought industry more directly into the clash with the mining sector.

World War II produced a lull in the mining-industry clash as Chilean copper entered a temporary boom period. But, as the balance of power began inevitably to shift toward the Chilean government, the income tax on the copper companies rose from 50 percent in 1945 to 70 percent in 1950, and in 1952 a state monopoly over all copper sales was established. The latter move was the first attempt at government intervention in copper marketing. But the failure of the state monopoly and decreased copper production created a renewed desire for a "good investment climate" and led to the "Neuvo Trato" (New Deal) Law of 1955.

The Neuvo Trato Law was a triumph for the copper companies and

marked another de-escalation of the industry-mining clash. The
principal gains of the companies were a stabilized tax base of 50
percent of income and an end to the artificial exchange controls.
This law followed a period when Chile's share of the world copper
market had been declining—a situation which the Chilean government
hoped new investment in the copper industry could correct. However,
the better incentives offered by the Nuevo Trato Law did not stimulate investment or production, since the multi-national corporations that controlled the Chilean copper industry still did not
view Chile as the most profitable area for future investments
(Moran, 1974:89-118). As it became evident that the law only increased company profits and did not produce increased investments,
the foreign corporations began to lose support in the Chilean government as well as in the private sector. Nationalization became
an inevitable result and was finally achieved under the Allende
regime in 1971.

The agriculture-industry clash in Chile has been much less
severe than that between industry and mining (Mamalakis, 1965:54-
59). One reason is that both these sectors are to a large extent
domestically owned, so neither is an easy target for nationalist
sentiments. Another reason is that the agricultural elite has
maintained a high political status and has successfully resisted
any major efforts to subvert its position. For example, land concentration was not threatened until the agrarian reform that was
pushed in the 1960s.[13] A final reason is that agricultural and
industrial elites have established many close family ties (Petras,
1972:39-40). The lack of any severe discrimination against agriculture is evident in Table 2.6 which shows that internal terms
of trade moved in a direction favorable to agriculture almost continuously from 1931 to 1954.

Agriculture's treatment has most nearly approximated that of
a neglected sector, especially since the mid- to late-1930s when
industry was emerging as the dominant sector (Mamalakis, 1965:
117-148; and Davis, 1963:390). The government, in its haste to
aid industry, has not given agriculture incentives to modernize
and certainly has not forced it to change its structure.

Table 2.6

Internal Terms of Trade--Chile
(Industrial Prices / Agricultural Prices)
1950 = 1.00

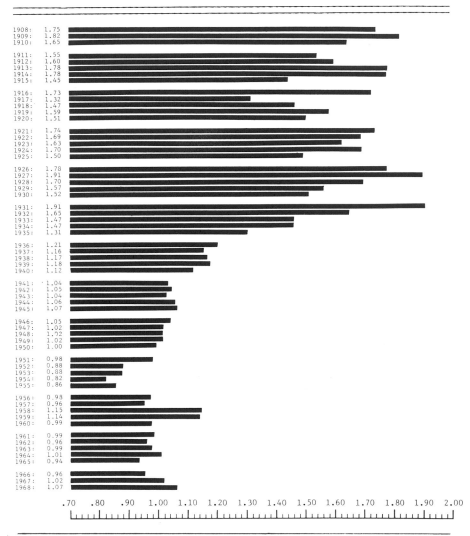

1908:	1.75
1909:	1.82
1910:	1.65
1911:	1.55
1912:	1.60
1913:	1.78
1914:	1.78
1915:	1.45
1916:	1.73
1917:	1.32
1918:	1.47
1919:	1.59
1920:	1.51
1921:	1.74
1922:	1.69
1923:	1.63
1924:	1.70
1925:	1.50
1926:	1.78
1927:	1.91
1928:	1.70
1929:	1.57
1930:	1.52
1931:	1.91
1932:	1.65
1933:	1.47
1934:	1.47
1935:	1.31
1936:	1.21
1937:	1.16
1938:	1.17
1939:	1.18
1940:	1.12
1941:	1.04
1942:	1.05
1943:	1.04
1944:	1.06
1945:	1.07
1946:	1.05
1947:	1.02
1948:	1.02
1949:	1.02
1950:	1.00
1951:	0.98
1952:	0.88
1953:	0.88
1954:	0.82
1955:	0.86
1956:	0.93
1957:	0.96
1958:	1.15
1959:	1.14
1960:	0.99
1961:	0.99
1962:	0.96
1963:	0.99
1964:	1.01
1965:	0.94
1966:	0.96
1967:	1.02
1968:	1.07

.70 .80 .90 1.00 1.10 1.20 1.30 1.40 1.50 1.60 1.70 1.80 1.90 2.00

Sources:
A. Ballesteros and Davis, 1963, p. 173.
B. Muñoz, 1971, p. 177.
C. United Nations Economic Commission for Latin America, The Process of Industrialization in Latin America, Statistical Annex, 1966.
D. Mamalakis, Markos J., 1967, Historical Statistics of Chile 1840-1967, pp. 255, 396.
E. Dirección de Estadística y Censos, Boletín.

INDUSTRIAL PRICES: 1908-14 and 1926-29 from A;
                     1915-25 and 1938-61 from B;
                     1930-37 from C;
                     1962-64 from D; and
                     1965-68 from E.

AGRICULTURAL PRICES: 1908-29 from A;
                     1930-40 from C;
                     1941-61 from D; and
                     1962-68 from E.

Table 2.7

Sectoral Production Indices--Chile
(1929 = 100)

	1929	1935	1940	1945	1950	1955	1960	1965	1969
Agriculture	100	97	108	118	122	137	133	146	167
Industry	100	117	143	246	275	320	352	502	592

SOURCES:
    1929-55: Ballesteros and Davis, 1963:160-61.
    1960-69: UNECLA, Statistical Bulletin for Latin America 1972.

Table 2.8

Ratio of Industrial Share of GNP to Agricultural Share of GNP
(1970)

Venezuela	Chile	Mexico	Argentina	Brazil
3.0	2.6	2.5	2.3	1.7

SOURCES: Tables 2.1, 2.4, 2.9, 2.11, and 2.13.

Table 2.9

Relative Productivity--Chile
(Percent of GNP / Percent of Labor Force)

	A Labor Force (%)	B GNP (%)	C A / B
1940			
Agriculture	37.3	14.9	0.40
Mining	5.7	8.6	1.50
Industry	17.4	16.7	0.96
Construction	3.5	2.3	0.66
Services	35.5	56.1	1.58
1945			
Agriculture	34.7	13.0	0.37
Mining	5.4	5.8	1.10
Industry	18.4	22.4	1.22
Construction	4.0	2.7	0.67
Services	36.8	59.3	1.61
1950			
Agriculture	32.2	13.2	0.41
Mining	5.0	5.7	1.10
Industry	19.3	21.9	1.13
Construction	4.7	2.4	0.51
Services	37.9	57.4	1.51
1955			
Agriculture	30.5	13.0	0.43
Mining	4.7	4.1	0.90
Industry	19.1	23.7	1.24
Construction	5.8	2.4	0.41
Services	38.9	54.1	1.39
1960			
Agriculture	30.7	11.3	0.37
Mining	4.0	6.4	1.60
Industry	17.8	19.2	1.08
Construction	5.6	2.4	0.43
Services	41.4	59.2	1.43
1965			
Agriculture	27.9	9.8	0.35
Mining	3.6	6.8	1.89
Industry	19.5	18.6	0.95
Construction	7.0	3.3	0.47
Services	41.5	58.5	1.41
1970			
Agriculture	23.2	9.2	0.40
Mining	3.5	10.0	2.86
Industry	19.9	24.2	1.22
Construction	6.3	4.6	0.73
Services	46.7	46.8	1.00

SOURCE: Markos J. Mamalakis, The Growth and Structure of the Chilean Economy, 1976, pp. 129, 155, 160, 165, 177.

Agriculture's rate of return has been consistently reduced by ceilings on agricultural prices (though the data of Table 2.6 call into question the success of such policies) and by exchange rate policies that have subsidized imports of competitive agricultural products (Mamalakis, 1965:117-20, 123-30). CORFO has favored industrial projects involving hydroelectric power, steel, and petroleum with its financing, while less than 4 percent of its credit or investment resources have been extended to agriculture (Mamalakis, 1965: 138-39; and Mamalakis, 1969b).

Since the neglect of the agricultural sector began in the 1930s, agricultural growth has continually lagged behind that of industry (see Table 2.7). During World War II industry surpassed agriculture in percent of GNP, and by 1970 industry's share was almost triple that of agriculture (see Table 2.8). Of the five countries in this study, Chile has the next-to-largest gap between agriculture and industry in terms of the ratio of industry's share of GNP to that of agriculture. Agriculture has remained the most backward sector in Chile, as evidenced by its relative productivity which has been around 0.40 since 1940 (see Table 2.9).

Mexico

Mexico is the clearest example of autonomously initiated sectoral clash in which an emerging industrial sector confronted the export elite and successfully challenged its control of the government and the economy. Autonomously initiated sectoral clash in Mexico was more intense than that in Brazil. The Mexican Revolution of 1910-20 cannot be totally explained as a result of sectoral clash, but conflict between the industrial sector and the agro-mining export sector in Mexico certainly was an important aspect of the Revolution. The major period of sectoral clash began in 1910 and continued until 1940, by which time the industrial sector had consolidated its dominant position.

The Mexican Revolution, directed against the ruling coalition of foreign interests and the agro-mining export elites, was fought by a variety of previously dispossessed groups, with the most well-known probably being the Mexican peasantry. In addition to the

role of the peasantry, an important component in the Revolution was
the struggle between sectoral elites. An aspiring political and
economic elite was as crucial to the revolutionary cause as were
the rural masses. The incipient industrial sector, both entrepreneurs and labor, supported the Revolution and benefited from it.
The role of entrepreneurs in general and the industrial sector in
particular in the Revolution is shown by the composition of the
Revolutionary leadership, the incorporation of private sector interest associations into the Revolutionary government, the policy
changes beneficial to industrialists, and the hostility of industrial labor to traditional forces associated with foreign interests
and the export elite.

The Revolution was begun by a growing, independent, and poli-
tically powerless segment of the entrepreneurial class. These entrepreneurs were centered in northern Mexico and included such
Revolutionary leaders are Francisco Madero, José María Maytorena,
Aaron Saenz, and Venustiano Carranza.[14] Many had suffered economically from pre-Revolutionary policies, and they concluded that they
could gain political power only by overthrowing the old order.[15]
Though lower-class support, particularly from the rural sector,
was crucial to the defeats of both Díaz and Huerta,[16] the leaders
emerging from the Revolution were hardly "representatives" of the
economically or socially dispossessed. Analysis of the delegates
to the 1917 Constitutional Convention shows that these were predominantly highly educated, middle-class professionals who had
been locked out of political power under Porfirio Díaz (Smith,
1973).

The links between the industrial sector and the Revolution
are particularly evident in the case of Francisco Madero. Through
his family's holdings, he had interests in both agriculture and
industry.[17] His identification with the industrial sector, particularly that segment involved in the processing of agrarian products, helped him to achieve his greatest electoral successes in
industrial and agro-industrial centers (Ruiz, 1976:6). Also, his
brother, Gustavo Madero, as an important textile mill owner as well
as a powerful voice in the new government, was a major link between

the industrialists and the Madero government. For example, Gustavo
Madero was instrumental in arranging meetings in 1912 between textile entrepreneurs and the government, in which the owners were
offered a tax reduction on textile goods in return for their acceptance of revised labor regulations (Ruiz, 1976:33-36).

Another indicator of the role of entrepreneurs is the fact
that private sector interest associations were organized for the
first time in 1917-18 and were thereby "incorporated to the Revolution."[18] A series of meetings convened in those years produced
the first industrial and commercial interest groups. These meetings also showed the "deep divisions between commerce and industry" (Shafer, 1973:30), and separate associations were organized
for these two sectors. Thus, sectoral clash was occurring even
at this stage between two business groups that were associated
with the Revolutionary government.

The government (principally the Minister of Labor, Commerce,
and Industry, Alfredo J. Pani, who acted with Carranza's approval)
called together the First National Congress of Merchants in July
191/ to study the "moralizaton" of commerce, the collective organization of chambers of commerce, means for developing domestic and
foreign commerce, and the high price of necessities. This Congress
evolved into the Confederation of National Chambers of Commerce
(Confederación de Cámaras Nacionales de Comercio, or CONCANACO;
see Shafer, 1973:22-25). In that same year, the Mexican Industrial
Center of Puebla took the initiative to ask the government to help
establish a national industrial organization in order to promote
the specific interests of industry.[19] Pani agreed and arranged a
Congress of Industrialists in November 1917 to deal with the organization of industrial chambers, means of promoting industrial
development, and industrial legislation. This Congress shortly
became the Confederation of Industrial Chambers (Confederación de
Cámara Industriales, or CONCAMIN; see Shafer, 1973:25-29).

A number of other policy changes in the revolutionary period
benefited industry and were partly a response to the support of
industrialists in the Revolution. In 1916 a protectionist tariff
was granted to jute and malt manufacturers, and in 1920 the

government stated for the first time that tariffs were for protectionist purposes (Ross and Christensen, 1959:29-31). A majority
of delegates of the 1917 Constitutional Convention supported the
establishment of a central bank, as did CONCANACO and CONCAMIN
(Shafer, 1973:28; and Smith, 1973:371, 391). In addition, the government announced tax relief for certain new industrial ventures in
1920 (Glade, 1963:85).

Industrialists also were to benefit from Article 27 of the 1917
Constitution which vested in the state the ownership of all subsoil
resources and gave the state the right to expropriate private land
and property.[20] This Article was directed at two sectoral enemies
of the industrialists: the agricultural elite and the foreign in-
vestors in such critical areas as petroleum and railroads. The economic nationalism symbolized by this Article was an integral part
of the rise of the industrial class in Mexico. According to William
Glade (1963:82), "the initiation of the industrial revolution in
Mexico was an implicit component of the economic nationalism with
which the Revolutionary program was imbued from the very outset."
The agrarian reform that stemmed from Article 27 had two consequences
that aided the industrialists: (1) the collapse of the power of
the largest and previously most influential hacendados; and (2) an
upswing in the mobility of rural workers.[21] The migration to the
cities that followed   reform provided the industrialists
with a wider labor market, and the redistributed wealth provided an
expanded domestic market.

Industrial labor was also an important supporter of the Revolution. The basis for their participation was their hostility to
the export elite and foreign owners, though they also clashed openly
with peasants at times.[22] Crucial strikes from 1906 to 1908, which
are sometimes referred to as the actual beginning of the Revolution,
were directed against industries that were either tied to the export
elite, were foreign-owned, or both.[23] Workers supported the vice-
presidential candidacy of General Bernardo Reyes in 1909, and upon
the repression of the reyista movement by Díaz, they supported Madero
in his electoral bid to defeat Díaz. When the Revolution broke out
in 1910, industrial workers were among the first revolutionary troops

from Sonora, Veracruz, Puebla, and the Federal District (R. Anderson, 1974:107-10; and Ruiz, 1976:5-16). Within the Revolutionary ranks the clash between labor and peasants was manifested in 1914 when the Red Battalions, made up almost entirely of workers from Mexico City and the state of Veracruz, fought with Carranza and Obregón against the peasant followers of Villa and Zapata (Ruiz, 1976:49-51).

The workers did not believe they were engaged in an anticapitalist struggle, but rather in a progressive fight against traditional and conservative forces. According to one author (R. Anderson, 1974:113), "workers who fought in or supported the Revolution against Díaz were defining their outrage in terms of demands for social justice they believed lawfully due them as Mexicans, not in terms of a heightened class consciousness." The workers were revolting against the old order dominated by rural and foreign interests, not against the industrial entrepreneurial class. This attitude of labor is additional evidence that the Revolution was more of a sectoral struggle than a class struggle.

The data on sectoral clash give some evidence of the improving position of industry in the post-Revolutionary period. In 1918 (the first year for which data are available) the relative position of industrial prices was at a very low point. In fact, industrial prices would never again sink this low relative to agricultural prices. Then in the next seven years, internal terms of trade moved to one of the most favorable levels for industrial goods. Though this was partially erased by a downward trend from 1927 to 1931, by 1931 industrial prices had rebounded to the 1924 level via-à-vis agricultural prices (see Table 2.10).

The industrial sector consolidated its position in the 1930s (Kaufman, 1977:212-12). Lázaro Cárdenas, President from 1934 to 1940, pursued two of the Revolution's main commitments--agrarian reform and nationalization--that were to the advantage of native industrialists. He redistributed almost 10 percent of Mexico's total land area, which was triple the area affected by previous land reform (Hansen, 1974:32-34), and he expropriated the

Table 2.10

Internal Terms of Trade--Mexico
(Industrial Prices / Agricultural Prices)
1954 = 1.00

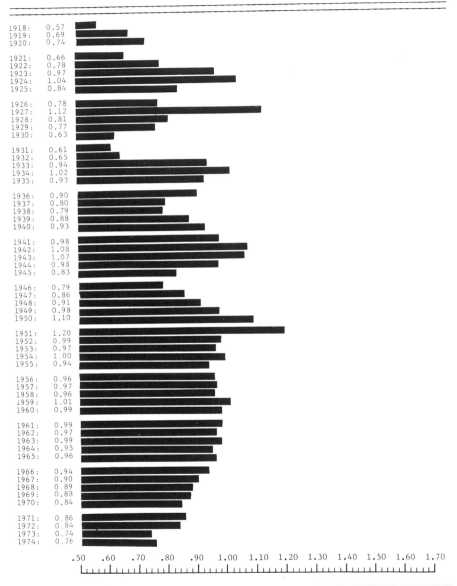

Year	Value
1918:	0.57
1919:	0.69
1920:	0.74
1921:	0.66
1922:	0.78
1923:	0.97
1924:	1.04
1925:	0.84
1926:	0.78
1927:	1.12
1928:	0.81
1929:	0.77
1930:	0.63
1931:	0.61
1932:	0.65
1933:	0.94
1934:	1.02
1935:	0.93
1936:	0.90
1937:	0.80
1938:	0.79
1939:	0.88
1940:	0.93
1941:	0.98
1942:	1.08
1943:	1.07
1944:	0.98
1945:	0.83
1946:	0.79
1947:	0.86
1948:	0.91
1949:	0.98
1950:	1.10
1951:	1.20
1952:	0.99
1953:	0.97
1954:	1.00
1955:	0.94
1956:	0.96
1957:	0.97
1958:	0.96
1959:	1.01
1960:	0.99
1961:	0.99
1962:	0.97
1963:	0.99
1964:	0.95
1965:	0.96
1966:	0.94
1967:	0.90
1968:	0.89
1969:	0.83
1970:	0.84
1971:	0.86
1972:	0.84
1973:	0.74
1974:	0.76

.50 .60 .70 .80 .90 1.00 1.10 1.20 1.30 1.40 1.50 1.60 1.70

Note:
    The price index for agricultural goods is taken from nonelaborated foodstuffs.
The price index for industrial goods is taken from: 1918-42, industrial production
goods; 1943-52, industrial primary materials; and 1953-74, elaborated primary materials.

Sources:
    1918-42: Dirección General de Estadística, Anuario Estadístico 1942 and 1943-45.
    1943-52: Dirección General de Estadística, Compendio Estadístico 1955.
    1953-74: Banco de Mexico, Informe Anual 1974.

foreign-owned petroleum companies and the major railroads. From
1930 to 1940 the industrial sector made greater gains in relative
productivity than in any other decade (see Table 2.11), so that in
1940 the Mexican industrial sector showed the highest relative productivity of all five countries in this study (see Table 2.5).
Table 2.11 shows that much of this increase is due to a displace-
ment of national product out of the mining and service sectors.
One can infer from this that Cárdenas' expropriation of the foreign-
owned petroleum sector contributed to this transfer.

In the 1940s industry surpassed agriculture in terms of percent of national product. Luciano Barraza's data (1969:85) on financial transfers in Mexico from 1942 to 1960 indicate that pesos
going into manufacturing exceeded those going out for the first time
in 1946. The positive balance for industry continued throughout
the time span of Barraza's data. His data also show (1969:86) that
public investment in manufacturing first exceeded that in agriculture in 1949 and that by 1960 public industrial investment was four
times greater than public agricultural investment.[24] Despite the
dominance of industry, since 1940 there have been no examples of
extreme suppression of a particular sector or of intermittent sectoral conflict that leads to economic crisis (Kaufman, 1977:212-13).
Thus, sectoral clash has not been a major factor in economic development in postwar Mexico. There were some policy differences
in the 1940s and 1950s between interest associations of commerce
and industry, but there have been just as important differences in
postwar period between different groups of industrial entrepreneurs.[25]

Venezuela

Venezuela is an intermediate case between state-initiated and
autonomously-initiated sectoral clash. The Venezuelan export sector is almost totally dominated by one mineral product, petroleum,
and until 1976 was foreign-owned. The clash with this sector is
definitely state-initiated, as the state has continually attempted
to increase its returns from and control over the petroleum industry. Also, clashes among the domestic economic sectors began in

Table 2.11

Relative Productivity—Mexico
(Percent of GNP / Percent of Labor Force)

	A Labor Force (%)	B GNP (%)	C A / B
1921			
Agriculture	76.0*	25.0*	0.33*
Mining			
Industry	12.0	22.0	1.83
Services	12.0	53.0	4.42
1930			
Agriculture	67.7	19.7	0.29
Mining	1.0	11.3	11.30
Industry	12.9	16.0	1.24
Services	14.4	53.0	3.68
1940			
Agriculture	65.4	22.1	0.34
Mining	1.8	7.7	4.28
Industry	10.9	20.3	1.86
Services	16.5	50.0	3.03
1950			
Agriculture	58.2	18.1	0.31
Mining	1.2	4.6	3.83
Industry	14.9	22.6	1.52
Services	21.5	55.2	2.57
1955			
Agriculture	57.8	17.8	0.31
Mining	1.2	4.1	3.42
Industry	14.7	23.1	1.57
Services	21.3	56.0	2.63
1960			
Agriculture	54.2	15.9	0.29
Mining	1.2	4.9	4.08
Industry	17.7	24.3	1.37
Services	26.2	55.9	2.13
1970			
Agriculture	39.2	11.6	0.30
Mining	1.4	4.7	3.36
Industry	21.5	29.5	1.37
Services	31.7	55.3	1.74

*Includes both agriculture and mining.

NOTE: Agriculture includes livestock and fishing. Industry includes manufacturing, construction, electricity, gas, and water. Services includes commerce, transportation, and communicaton.

SOURCES: All 1921 data are from Goldsmith (1966:72). All other labor force data are from the International Labor Office, International Yearbook of Labor Statistics. All other GNP data are from United Nations Economic Commission for Latin America, Statistical Bulletin for Latin America 1972.

the 1960s and have been related to government economic policies, which is characteristic of state-initiated clash.

Yet there are also signs in Venezuela of sectoral clash that is independent of the state. In the first place, the state has not predominantly favored any one sector. Since World War II, industrialization has been a major concern of state policy, but neither agriculture nor commerce have been suppressed or neglected. The sectoral clash that has occurred in the 1960s and 1970s among the domestic sectors has not involved an alliance between the state and one sector against the other sectors, but rather has involved conflicts among the sectors themselves. This has occurred primarily within the all-encompassing interest association of the private sector: the Federation of Chambers and Associations of Commerce and Industry (Federación Venezolana de Cámaras y Asociaciones de Comercio y Producción, or FEDECAMARAS). Finally, especially since the mid-1960s, there has been increasing antagonism between the state and all economic sectors. Thus, one of the most crucial clashes in Venezuela is between the public and private sectors.

Petroleum is even more important to the Venezuelan economy than copper is to the Chilean economy. In recent years, petroleum has represented as much as 95 percent of all export earnings, over 35 percent of total national output, and has been the source of about 85 percent of total government revenue. Oil production began in earnest in Venezuela in the 1920s, and by 1929 petroleum had become the main export commodity (over 75 percent of total exports). Yet only 10 percent of the petroleum income was remaining in Venezuela at this time (Feinstein, 1965:12). So when dictatorial president Juan Vicente Goméz died in 1935, there was much room for expansion of the state's share of petroleum wealth.

The government-petroleum clash began in 1938 with a new concessions law that increased the royalty rate and other surface and exploration taxes. Since that time, all Venezuelan governments have aimed to increase the public share of oil income, even though the willingness of regimes to antagonize the foreign oil companies in doing so has varied.[26] In the postwar period, taxes on the petroleum industry have steadily increased, with the greatest rise in 1958. After experimenting with a policy of active control over the oil companies in the early 1960s, in the mid- to late-1960s the government took a more accommodating stance toward the companies, particularly in the 1966 tax compromise and the 1968 desulfuriza- tion agreement.[27] In the 1970s, however, with the domestic private sector no longer supporting the foreign petroleum companies, nation- alization became a foregone conclusion and was accomplished in 1976. Yet despite the escalating conflict between the petroleum industry and the state, the Venezuelan economy has not diversified and re- mains as dependent upon petroleum as ever.

Despite a commitment to promote industrial growth, which was emphasized especially after 1958, the agricultural sector has not been repressed or even ignored by the government. Government sup- port programs for agriculture began in 1934 with direct subsidies and preferential exchange rates for the two major agricultural ex- port crops (coffee and cacao) and have continued through present-day administrations. In 1937 a colonization program was initiated to establish medium-sized units in commercial agriculture, and in 1940 irrigation projects became a major item in the federal budget (Fein- stein, 1965:55-59). Direct aid programs to agriculture through the Venezuelan Development Corporation (CVF) were stressed from its in- ception in 1946 until 1958, and CVF-sponsored projects have been especially important in contributing to increases in rice and sugar production (Rollins, 1955:87). The credits, subsidies, preferential exchange rates, and the other policies supporting agricultural growth have continued throughout the postwar period.[28] Most re- cently, President Carlos Andrés Peréz has proclaimed the backward state of Venezuela's agricultural sector to be the nation's great- est major problem and the first priority of his government. Evi- dence of the benefits possibly derived from these government support programs is given in Table 2.12, which shows that internal terms of trade turns in agriculture's favor from 1941 to 1947 and remained quite stable after that.

It would appear then that conflicts among domestic sectors in Venezuela have largely been circumvented by state policies giving benefits to both agriculture and industry. Yet since 1960 small

Table 2.12

Internal Terms of Trade--Venezuela
(Industrial Prices / Agricultural Prices)
1956-57 = 1.00

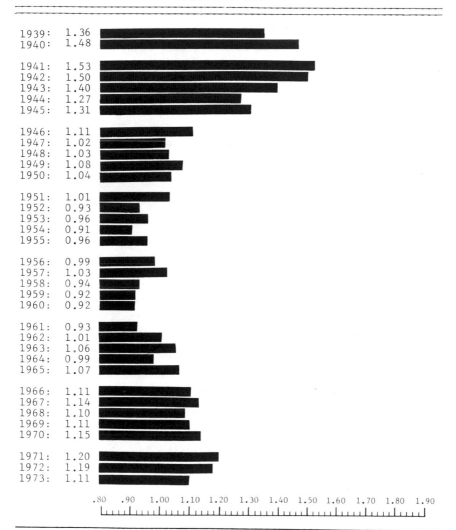

Year	Value
1939:	1.36
1940:	1.48
1941:	1.53
1942:	1.50
1943:	1.40
1944:	1.27
1945:	1.31
1946:	1.11
1947:	1.02
1948:	1.03
1949:	1.08
1950:	1.04
1951:	1.01
1952:	0.93
1953:	0.96
1954:	0.91
1955:	0.96
1956:	0.99
1957:	1.03
1958:	0.94
1959:	0.92
1960:	0.92
1961:	0.93
1962:	1.01
1963:	1.06
1964:	0.99
1965:	1.07
1966:	1.11
1967:	1.14
1968:	1.10
1969:	1.11
1970:	1.15
1971:	1.20
1972:	1.19
1973:	1.11

.80 .90 1.00 1.10 1.20 1.30 1.40 1.50 1.60 1.70 1.80 1.90

Note:
    Industrial price index is for elaborated products. Agri-
cultural price index is for unelaborated farm products.

Sources:
    1939-55: Banco Central de Venezuela, Memoria 1957.
    1956-59: Banco Central de Venezuela, Informe Económico 1965.
    1960-69: Banco Central de Venezuela, Informe Económico 1969.
    1969-73: Banco Central de Venezuela, Informe Económico 1973.

and large industrialists, commercial businessmen, and agricultural interests have clashed over various issues within the structure of FEDECAMARAS (J.A. Gil, 1977:141, 146-48). These clashes have occurred over three policy issues: import substitution, agricultural development, and regional economic integration. The state has initiated important changes in each of these areas, and the private sectors have responded to protect their own interests.[29] These divisions within FEDECAMARAS have at times prevented it from exerting a strong influence (Levy, 1968:39; and Blank, 1973:238). The cohesiveness of the organization has only been preserved by three structural characteristics of the private sector: (1) the oligopolistic nature of all sectors;[30] (2) a large number of entrepreneurs with capital invested in two or more different sectors (Blank, 1971:93; and Bond, 1975:80); and (3) a common mistrust of the growing economic role of the state.[31]

Throughout the 1960s Venezuela was only minimally involved in Latin American economic integration schemes, and the principal opponent of integration was FEDECAMARAS. But from 1963 to 1965 FEDECAMARAS was sharply divided over this issue. Leading the opposition to Venezuela's proposed membership in the Latin American Free Trade Association (LAFTA) were the agricultural interests, followed closely by the small industrialists and bankers; the large-scale industrialists, because they were associated with less labor-intensive enterprises and could more readily compete on a regional basis, were those most in favor of integration (Clark, 1971; and Blank, 1973:238). The agrarian and small industrial interests won out in 1965, and FEDECAMARAS was able to postpone Venezuelan entry to LAFTA until 1966 and to gain key stipulations for continuing a certain level of protection in Venezuela.

The debate over import substitution has pitted industry, which favors greater government tariff protection for its products, versus commerce, which prefers lower tariffs and less restricted trade (Bond, 1975:75-78, 100-02). This conflict over tariff policy is potentially the most damaging for FEDECAMARAS, since industry and commerce together account for 76 percent of its member groups and both sectors are well-organized internally. Because most

members recognize the need for industrialization, industry's opinion
has generally prevailed and government policy has favored high tariffs. In another area, industry and commerce have been allied
against the agricultural sector over the government's attempts to
develop Venezuela's backward agriculture through subsidies, tariff
protection, and public investment (Bond, 1975:78, 102). Tariff
protection for agricultural products has hurt industry and commerce,
and agricultural subsidies and investment have deprived other sectors of these resources. This conflict has escalated to the point
that in 1972 a federation of eighty-two agricultural groups,
FEDEAGRO, withdrew from FEDECAMARAS, while nineteen agricultural
groups stayed.

A principal reason for these clashes is the major gap that
exists between agriculture and the other sectors. As evidence of
this, Table 2.8 shows that the Venezuelan ratio of industrial share
of GNP to agricultural share is the largest of the five countries.
More than any other sector in that nation, Venezuelan agriculture
has resisted modernization. One author (Feinstein, 1965:44) even
says that the transition from subsistence and latifundista agriculture to efficient, commercial production·has not taken place in
Venezuela, though data in Table 2.13 show that the relative productivity of agriculture has improved markedly in the 1960s. It is
certainly true that agricultural growth has lagged behind that of
industry and other sectors. Charles Rollins (1955) estimates that
agriculture generated the smallest share of the increase in GNP
from 1936 to 1952 (2 percent, compared to 17 percent for manufacturing), and Table 2.14 shows that in the 1950s agriculture's
growth rate was almost one-third that of industry's and continued
to be lower throughout the 1960s. The slow rates of growth for
agriculture, the continued concentration of land ownership, and
the low levels of private investment in agriculture indicate that
government policies to stimulate agricultural development have met
with little success.

The final area of economic cleavage is that between the state
as an economic actor and the private sector. The Venezuelan state
has grown increasingly powerful in the economic sphere through its

Table 2.13

Relative Productivity--Venezuela
(Percent of GNP / Percent of Labor Force)

	A Labor Force (%)	B GNP (%)	C A / B
1950			
Agriculture	41.3	8.0	0.19
Mining	2.6	31.0	11.90
Industry	15.7	16.0	1.02
Services	31.9	45.0	1.41
1961			
Agriculture	32.1	7.0	0.22
Mining	1.9	29.1	15.30
Industry	18.7	17.6	0.94
Services	40.8	46.3	1.13
1970			
Agriculture	21.8	7.1	0.33
Mining	2.0	18.6	9.30
Industry	25.5	21.4	0.84
Services	49.3	52.9	1.07

NOTE: Agriculture includes livestock and fishing. Industry includes manufacturing, construction, electricity, gas, and water.
Services include commerce, transportation, and communications.
Labor force percentages do not add to 100 because the remaining
share was not classifiable.

SOURCES: All labor force data are from the International Labor
Office, International Yearbook of Labor Statistics. GNP data for
1950 and 1961 are from United Nations Economic Commission for Latin
America, Statistical Bulletin for Latin America 1972. GNP data for
1970 are from Banco Central de Venezuela, Informe Económico 1973.

Table 2.14

Sectoral Growth Rates--Venezuela
(in percentages)

	Industry	Agriculture	Total
1959 - 59	162	62	105
1960 - 69	83	53	65

SOURCES: Banco Central de Venezuela, Memoria and Informe Económico.

enormous revenues from petroleum and its recent acquisition of ownership of that industry; as a result, the private sector has become
more hostile to the public sector. As was stated above, fear of
state economic power was one of the reasons behind the creation of
FEDECAMARAS (see note 31 here). Disagreements between the state
and the private sector have become more salient since the mid-1960s.
In 1965 FEDECAMARAS first announced its opposition to Leoni's plan
to join LAFTA, and in 1967 FEDECAMARAS even more vigorously opposed
Venezuela's entry into another regional integration plan, the Andean
Pact (Bond, 1975:217-71). Also, FEDECAMARAS strongly opposed the
1966 tax reform, which Bond (1975:171) calls "one of the most bit-
terly contested issues of public policy in the short history of
Venezuela's democratic government."

Conclusion

Figure 2.1 arrays these five countries along a spectrum from
autonomously initiated sectoral clash to state-initiated sectoral
clash. Sectoral clash in Argentina exhibited the greatest degree
of state involvement. Perón's policies that discriminated against
the agro-export sector were primarily responsible for the transfer
of resources among sectors, though this strategy stressed the suppression of the export sector more than the dominance of the industrial sector. Chilean sectoral clash was also state-initiated
and relied on economic policies to transfer resources from the
mining-export sector to the industrial sector. In neither

Figure 2.1

Who Initiates Sectoral Clash
(Dates in which sectoral clash was most
intense are in parentheses.)

Autonomously initiated				State-initiated
Mexico (1910–40)	Brazil (1920–40)	Venezuela (1958–76)	Chile (1939–71)	Argentina (1946–55)

Argentina nor Chile did industrial entrepreneurs clash with other sectors outside the sphere of state policy, nor did they exert strong pressures on the state to enact such policies. The intermediate case of Venezuela is similar to Chile in that both involved state-initiated suppression of a foreign-owned mining enclave, but Venezuela also has experienced sectoral clashes within FEDECAMARAS that are relatively independent of state interference and a growing cleavage between the private sector and the state.

In Brazil and Mexico--the clearest examples of autonomous roles of entrepreneurs in sectoral clash--political and economic conflicts among sectors emerged that were quite independent of the role of the state. Industrialists in Brazil began to form separate associational groups as early as 1880, and the major political and economic break with traditional agrarian and commercial interests occurred in the 1920s. The Mexican Revolution was partly an instance of sectoral clash initiated autonomously, as displaced entrepreneurial groups led the revolt against the traditional oligarchy. Both industrial entrepreneurs and industrial labor generally supported the Revolution, and at times they exhibited major differences with other sectors (CONCAMIN vs. CONCANACO and the Red Battalions vs. the peasants).

As expected, autonomously initiated sectoral clash occurred earlier than state-initiated clash. The major period of conflict between the emerging industrial sector and the traditional export sector in Brazil and Mexico was from 1910 or 1920 to 1940, while state policies to transfer resources out of the export sector in Argentina, Chile, and Venezuela were not instituted until after 1940. A plausible conclusion is that state-initiated clash was delayed, especially in Argentina and Chile where the timing of industrial growth and import substitution was roughly comparable to that in Brazil and Mexico. In Argentina and Chile, industrial entrepreneurs and the state eventually had to take the initiative. This failure of industrial entrepreneurs to initiate the conflict with the export sector meant that sectoral clash due to state policies would be relatively late.

The extent of foreign ownership in the export sector has been hypothesized as relating to crucial aspects of development, and there are some interesting differences among these five countries in terms of ownership of the export sector (Cardoso and Faletto, 1973). Chile, Mexico, and Venezuela had extensive foreign ownership in the export sector at the time of sectoral clash, and the export sectors in Argentina and Brazil were largely domestically owned. One could expect that a foreign-dominated export sector would be an easy target for discrimination, but this distinction does not appear to be related to the different types of sectoral clash. The three countries with extensive foreign ownership represent three different positions on the spectrum of "who initiates" the clash.

Another important characteristic of the export sector is the degree to which it is an enclave, i.e., its geographic concentration and its dependence on one or two primary products. One could also expect that an export enclave would make an easy target for sectoral clash, though enclaves might control enough economic and political power to resist any challenges. Including the dichotomy between enclave and non-enclave export sectors slightly improves the relationship with sectoral clash, since the Mexican export sector was diversified geographically and economically, while the export sectors in Chile and Venezuela were both concentrated in a small geographic region and in one product. Argentina and Brazil are intermediate cases in terms of export enclaves, with a moderate degree (greater than Mexico but less than Chile or Venezuela) of geographic concentration and dependence on one or two export products. Thus, even though the degree to which the export sector exists in an enclave setting comes closer to explaining patterns of sectoral clash than the degree of foreign ownership, neither variable matches the distinctions between autonomously initiated and state-initiated sectoral clash very well (see Table 2.15).

Table 2.15

Characteristics of the Export Sector and Sectoral Clash

| | Export Sector | | Sectoral Clash |
	Foreign Ownership?	Enclave?	Autonomously initiated?
ARGENTINA	no	somewhat	no
BRAZIL	no	somewhat	yes
CHILE	yes	yes	no
MEXICO	yes	no	yes
VENEZUELA	yes	yes	somewhat

<u>Notes</u>

[1]Data for internal terms of trade show the ratio of industrial prices to agricultural prices or, more specifically, the number of units of goods one sector must give up to receive one unit of goods from the other sector. Trends in domestic terms of trade are usually the result of either government policies favoring one sector or relative changes in the level of efficiency, resources, or demand for products between sectors. These data should reflect the movements of relative strength and weakness between sectors. If internal terms of trade are decreasing, the industrial sector will receive fewer units of agricultural goods for the same number of units of industrial goods. It should be stressed that the absolute figures in these data have no meaning except when compared across time. Base points of 1.00 are set arbitrarily and do not imply equal terms of trade. Thus, in Argentina the values of 0.76 for 1926 and 1.00 for 1960 could be rescaled to read 1.00 for 1926 and 1.32 for 1960. The point is that internal terms of trade improved substantially in favor of the industrial sector between 1926 and 1960.

The other measure of sectoral clash presented here--relative productivity--is the ratio of percent of GNP in a sector or combination of sectors to its percent of the total labor force. Mamalakis (1971a) uses this measure as his principal indicator of sectoral clash, because he claims it shows a sector's capacity to generate a resource surplus. The greater the disparities among data for relative productivity in a single year, the greater the inequality among sectors. Also, changes through time in relative productivity in a sector should indicate improvements in the overall position of that sector.

[2]In the 1920s, marginal national capitalists, immigrants, and U.S. capital did begin to dispute the primacy of British and agrarian interests in Argentina, but no real threat was posed to the hegemony of the British and agro-export elites. See Corradi (1974: 350-51).

[3]On the close historical ties between industrialists and the agrarian oligarchy, see Polit (1968:309-404, 411-14).

[4]It is clear that industrialists opposed the Roca-Runciman Treaty. One of the earliest manifestations of an agriculture-industry clash was a demonstration on June 12, 1933 in Buenos Aires where some 70,000 workers defended the industrial sector by protesting the recent Treaty which they felt sacrificed the nation's industrial strength in favor of the interests of the agro-livestock groups (Freels, 1968:32-33). This demonstration was organized by the national organization of industrialists (the Argentine Industrial Union, or UIA) and was the first and the <u>only</u> time the UIA participated with subordinate groups in an alliance against the agro-export oligarchy (Murmis and Portantiero, 1971:16-19).

[5]In this Plan, which organized industrial interests strongly

supported, Federico Pinedo's objective was the preservation of the export oligarchy through the achievement of a degree of industrial expansion so as to lessen the economy's vulnerability. Even so, the two organized agrarian interest groups (the Confederation of Rural Associations and the Rural Society) opposed this Plan and soundly defeated it (Freels, 1968:18-19; and Murmis and Portantiero, 1971:33-42).

[6]See Toledo (1977); Latin America Political Report, June 3, 1977 and January 13, 1978; and Latin America Economic Report, April 29 and June 17, 1977, and January 13 and 20, 1978.

[7]Dean (1969:67-69). Also Leff (1968:114-15) says that industrialists emerged in a context of conflict with other sectors and that this conflict actually was a detriment to the political influence of industrialists, especially in the Congress.

[8]For more detailed descriptions of the CIESP, see Dean (1969:139-48) and Schmitter (1971:147-48).

[9]See Leff (1968:12-14), Dean (1969:181-206), and Wirth (1970:17-68).

[10]See Dean (1969:186-94), Wirth (1970:18, 47-50), and Harding (1973:75-76). Kaufman (1977:200, 213) says that coffee and manufacturing interests generally converged in these years, but he seems to ignore the anti-industrial bias in the economic policies before 1937. The most plausible argument here is that the defense of coffee export prices also maintained domestic demand and spurred some new industrial investments (Furtado, 1971:193-224; and Cardoso and Faletto, 1973:78-82, 116-22).

[11]On the postwar export policy and the overvaluation, see Leff (1967; and 1968:14-27, 77-83), Bergsman (1970:27-54), and Bergsman and Malan (1971:114-15).

[12]Theodore Moran (1974) and Franklin Tugwell (1975b) describe the cases of Chile and Venezuela, respectively, as models of incremental escalation of the conflict between the host country and the foreign-owned export enclave.

[13]Petras (1972:17-18, 260-63) and F. Gil (1966:76-77). Despite its high political and social status, the economic dominance of the landed elite was ended by the ascension of the mining export sector and foreign investment beginning in the late nineteenth century. Taxes on the export sector allowed the traditional oligarchy to maintain political power, as government income, mostly from taxes on foreign trade, tripled from 1879 to 1887 (Wallis, 1970:42). But the economic center of Chile shifted from the land to the mines and from domestic capital to foreign capital. As James Petras (1972:87) describes the situation in the late nineteenth century, the Chilean landed elite "kept the reins of power, but no longer owned the horse."

[14]Madero, of course, began the Revolution that overthrew Porfirio Díaz in 1911 and was president of Mexico from 1911 to 1913; Maytorena was an early follower of Madero; and Carranza was president of Mexico from 1914 to 1919 and established the 1917 Constitution. Saenz was a revolutionary turned industrialist who had important ties to two presidents in the 1920s: Alvaro Obregón and Plutarco Elías Calles (Hamilton, 1977:17-26).

[15]See Cumberland (1952:56), Cockroft (1968:62-63), Hu-Dehart (1974:92-93), and F. Katz (1974:45-47). Also, Clark Reynolds (1970:25-26) describes how export-led growth by 1910 had sown the seeds of political instability by limiting industrial growth.

[16]Porfirio Díaz was president of Mexico from 1876 to 1911, and Victoriano Huerta was a military dictator who ruled Mexico from February 1913 to July 1914.

[17]Ross (1955:3), Cockroft (1968:61-63), and Ruiz (1976:28).

[18]These were the words of Alfredo J. Pani, Carranza's Minister of Labor, Commerce, and Industry, as quoted in Shafer (1973:22).

[19]It is perhaps significant that the government initiated the call for a commercial association, while industrialists initiated the contact with the government in order to organize an industrial association. The commercial entrepreneurs were much stronger than the industrial entrepreneurs, but the industrialists were determined to protect their separate interests.

[20]Hansen (1974:89-90). Shafer (1973:28) does point out, however, that at the first Congress of Industrialists there were some fears expressed concerning state ownership of land and subsoil resources. Apparently the industrial entrepreneurs at this time were not as hostile to foreign interests as was industrial labor. Industrialists did not express strong nationalist sentiments until the 1940s.

[21]See Barraza (1969:73-75), González Casanova (1970:48-49), and Hansen (1974:31-39). One of the strongest exponents of the linkage between the agrarian and the industrial aspects of the Revolution is Manuel Germán Parra who states (1967:86) that "the agrarian revolution and the industrial revolution in Mexico are not two antagonistic acts, but rather two aspects of the same phenomenon [the Mexican Revolution]."

[22]On the hostility of industrial labor to foreign owners, managers, and workers, see Ruiz (1976:11-16). F. Katz (1974:45-46) stresses the important role of displaced workers in northern Mexico in the Revolution.

[23]These refer to the 1906 uprising of copper miners at Cananea, the 1907 textile workers strike at Rio Blanco, and the railroad strike of 1908. The copper industry and the railroads were both

linked to the export sector, and all three industries were primarily foreign-owned. See Ruiz (1976:17-25).

[24] Industry also has been fairly independent of agriculture in terms of new investment. Around 1970, only about 15 percent of new outside industrial investment came from agriculture (Derossi, 1971: 153-59).

[25] On the differences between commercial and industrial associations, see Shafer (1973:55-56, 60-61, 114, 117-20).

[26] Franklin Tugwell (1975b:144-75) says the state's leverage vis-à-vis the foreign oil companies has been determined by the natural shift in the balance of power between the host government and the foreign companies as well as by the "learning rate" of the host government. For other reviews of Venezuelan petroleum policy, see Feinstein (1965), Edwards (1971), and Harris (1971).

[27] In 1966 the government had decided to overhaul the tax structure and increase the burden of the private sector—both domestic and foreign. The foreign oil companies struck a bargain with the government that is generally believed to have been to the companies' favor, while the Venezuelan private sector was left alone in opposition to the tax reform. In 1968 the government relaxed investment restrictions so that Standard Oil of New Jersey's subsidiary could establish a desulfurization plant. See Tugwell (1975b:88-99).

[28] However, Strassman (1964:182--citing Lieuwen, 1961:64-88, 105-09) does state that in 1958 President Betancourt pressed landowners hard but took a more moderate view toward private industry.

[29] José Antonio Gil (1975:60-61) maintains that these economic policies have developed not because entrepreneurs have pressed for them (though they have), but rather because the government unilaterally decided to pursue them. Entrepreneurs then have had the most success in delaying or redefining the issues.

[30] Rangel (1972:49-65 and 271-308), J.A. Gil (1975:26-27), and Tugwell (1975b:28-32).

[31] Robert Bond (1975:59) says that this mistrust of state economic power also played a part in the creation of FEDECAMARAS in 1944.

Chapter 3

INDUSTRIALIZATION POLICIES AND SECTORAL CLASH

This chapter focuses on the timing and emphasis of industrialization policies in relation to the major periods of sectoral clash.
It was suggested in the Introduction that autonomously initiated
clash was more likely to precede the most significant period of
industry-promoting policies and to contribute to policies stressing
integrated industrial growth. On the other hand, state-initiated
sectoral clash was suggested as more likely to coincide with the
most significant period of industry-promoting policies and to hin-
der policies that stress integrated industrial growth. In this
chapter we will discuss industrialization policies and examine these
expectations regarding the relationships between policies and sectoral clash.

The industrialization policies to be described here fall under
the broad categories of industrial protectionism and industrial promotion (UNECLA, 1966:155-86). Protectionist policies include foreign exchange policies, tariff policies, and other measures affecting foreign trade. Promotion policies include credit and investment policies, taxation policies, and other measures encouraging
national industrial development. Particularly for the protectionist
policies, two periods can usually be identified: (1) a period when
such policies are intended as temporary responses to balance of payments crises; and (2) a period when such policies are designed to
specifically encourage industrialization.[1] As might be expected,
most promotion policies are instituted during the latter period of
protectionist policies. This phase, when policies are deliberately
designed to promote industrial growth, is the one that will be compared to the timing of sectoral clash.

An important aspect of industrialization policies is the degree
to which they emphasize integrated and diversified industrial growth.

In Latin America, industrialization policies initially stress the import substitution of consumer goods (also referred to as light industry), but they do not always progress so as to encourage the import substitution of capital goods (also referred to as heavy or basic industry). This progression of emphasis from consumer goods to capital goods is what is meant by "integrated and diversified" industrial growth. Some authors refer to this as "backward-linking import substitution" because capital goods are one of the most important inputs of light industries (Hirschman, 1968:17-24). As well as discussing the timing of industrialization policies, Chapter 3 will describe the degree to which policies promote backward-linking import substitution.

Argentina

Argentine economic policies began taking on a semblance of protectionism in the 1930s. Economic nationalism and protectionism were especially strong from 1930 to 1932 when Lieutenant General Uriburu served as Provisional President. Policy initiatives included currency depreciation from 1929 to 1931, tariff increases in 1931 and 1932, and the creation of the Exchange Control Commission in 1931, which immediately devalued the peso by almost 40 percent from its 1929 parity.[2] Despite the devaluation, exchange control after 1931 still left the peso at an overvalued rate which reduced the income of the agrarian groups, whose output was largely exported, and subsidized the importation of raw materials and capital goods (Ferrer, 1967:169-74).

Yet these policies that seemed to favor industrialists were short-lived, and most of the Uriburu policies had been reversed by the mid-1930s. Overall, the industrialization policies instituted in the 1930s were primarily a response to the economic crisis of the Depression and represented only an adjustment of the old economic structure in the direction of industrialization controlled by the rural elites (Polit, 1968:413-14; and Jorge, 1971:17-41, 107-29). These policies increased effective protection very little, and the same industries that were favored with the highest tariffs before 1930, primarily in consumer goods, continued to be favored in the late 1930s (Chu, 1972:21-28). There was no contradiction between the

industrial orientation of the government and the interests of the
most powerful segment of the landed elite, as the government policies promoted a form of "industrial growth without an industrial
revolution."[3] The emphasis was on the production of non-durable
consumer goods and not on the installation of the basic industries.
These consumer goods used domestic raw materials and thus contributed to the demand for rural sector products. Industrial expansion
took advantage of existing capacity and did not diversify the structure of the internal market. The focus was only on those industrial
branches that were most closely integrated with the agrarian economy
and that posed no threat to the existing hierarchy of economic and
political power.

In the late 1930s industrialization policies began to be emphasized once again. In 1938 the official exchange rate was finally
devalued and the system of prior exchange permits was extended to all
imports; in 1939 the free market exchange rate was abolished for
merchandise imports, and two official rates for imports were created in its place. The Trade Promotion Corporation, the precursor
to the IAPI, was created in 1941 with authority over foreign exchange transactions (Salaberren, et al., 1946:121).

Still, the most important industrialization policies did not
appear until after the 1943 coup brought nationalistic military
officers to power. Decree 14630 in June 1944 empowered the executive to protect and promote new industries of national importance
by increasing import duties up to 50 percent, by applying quotas
on imports that compete with local products, and by granting subsidies to industries crucial to the national defense (Wythe, 1949:
126; and Altimir, et al., 6, no. 21:114-35--see note 18 here).
Another important law in March 1947 again authorized the executive
to increase duties as much as 50 percent and to impose duties up
to 25 percent on goods formerly duty-free (Wythe, 1949:127). From
1948 to 1950 protectionism increased through greater import restrictions and currency devaluations (Schwartz, 1969:272-79). The increased emphasis on protectionism is seen in data on the effective
rate of protection, which was only 34 percent in 1927, 38 percent
in 1937, 44 percent in 1946, 188 percent in 1950, and 291 percent

in 1954 (Chu, 1972:26-27).

Other significant policy initiatives in the area of industrial promotion occurred in this period as well. The Bank of Industrial Credit was established in 1944 to give more emphasis to manufacturing credits, and between 1945 and 1948 the government endorsed substantial credit expansion for industry at negative real rates of interest (Schwartz, 1968:269-72). The nationalism of the Central Bank in 1946 also was a boost to industrial credit (Salaberren, et al., 1951:161; and Freels, 1968:43). Public sector direct investment and ownership in industrial enterprises became significant in the postwar period (Altimir, et al, 6, no. 22-23:469-87). The first step in this direction was the organization of the Dirección General de Fabricaciones Militares (DGFM) in 1941 to promote the manufacture of war equipment. Then in 1947 the Dirección Nacional de Industrias del Estado (DINIE) was created to coordinate the establishment of state ownership in certain industries, and in 1952 the Dirección Nacional de Fabricaciones y Investigaciones Aeronauticas (DINFIA) was begun. Eventually, the DGFM controlled fourteen state enterprises; DINFIA, eleven; and DINIE, thirty-eight (UNECLA, 1966:174). Also, SOMISA, the state-owned steel company that was administered by the armed forces, was originally approved in 1947, though it did not begin production until 1961 (Díaz Alejandro, 1971).

One of the major characteristics of these industrialization policies was the lack of emphasis on capital goods industries (Díaz Alejandro, 1970:254-69). The Peronist industrialization policies throughout the 1940s continued to stress the same type of consumer goods and light industries that had been promoted by the agriculture-industry alliance in the 1930s, and the few heavy industrial projects being pushed were primarily under the supervision of the military (Kenworthy, 1972:19-20; and Mallon and Sourrouille, 1975: 12, 75-76). Import substitution of consumer goods had progressed substantially in the 1930s, primarily due to exogenous factors, yet the government in the 1940s began belatedly promoting these same areas of import substitution. From the standpoint of industrial progress, these policies were obviously late and misdirected. By the end of World War II the light industries needed the competitive

Figure 3.1

Summary of Argentine Industrialization Policies, 1930-55

Date	Policy	Emphasis
1930-32	devaluation	consumer goods
	tariff increase	consumer goods
	exchange control	consumer goods
1938-41	devaluation	consumer goods
	exchange control	consumer goods
	DGFM (public investment)	capital goods
1944	protection (import tariffs and quotas) and promotion (subsidies) for new industries	consumer goods
	Bank of Industrial Credit (credit expansion)	consumer goods
1946	nationalization of Central Bank (credit expansion)	consumer goods
1947	tariff increase	consumer goods
	DINIE (public investment)	capital goods
1948-50	import restrictions	consumer goods
	devaluation	consumer goods
1952	DINFIA (public investment)	capital goods
1953-55	protection de-emphasized	

push of reduced protection to insure their efficiency, while the
heavy industries which had not experienced much import substitution
were those most deserving government promotion and protection (Díaz
Alejandro, 1970:106-26). However, from the standpoint of Perón and
his major supporters, it made sense to favor light industry because
of the ability of these industries to produce employment and to
satisfy consumption needs of the working class. Díaz Alejandro
(1970:126) aptly summarizes the rationale of Perón: "Peronist policies present a picture of a government interested not so much in industrialization as in a nationalistic and populist policy of increasing the real consumption, employment, and economic security of the
masses--and of the new entrepreneurs."

Only after 1953 did the emphasis of protectionist policies
switch from light to heavy industries.[4] Basic industries were particularly promoted during the Frondizi administration from 1958 to
1962 through protectionist policies, public investment, and a wider
acceptance of the necessity to attract foreign capital. Though industrialization policies overall were becoming less significant,
their focus was more on basic industries in which import substitution could still be achieved.

Brazil

Pro-industrialization policies in Brazil were not initiated
until the late 1930s, and the most deliberate period of protectionism and promotion for industry was not until after World War
II. Vargas' early administration (1930-37) stressed the recovery
of the export sector through an economic policy that focused on the
governmental purchase of the coffee surplus in order to restrict
supply artificially and to boost prices. Though Brazil adopted the
customary policies to reduce imports after the onset of the Depression (exchange control, import restrictions, and protective tariffs),
these were designed only to reduce balance of payments tensions and
were relaxed somewhat beginning in 1934 (Dean, 1969:196-206; and
Wirth, 1970:21).

Government policy slowly recognized the increasing influence
of industry, and in the late 1930s a government industrial program
started to evolve. Along with imposing the Estado Novo on Brazil,

Vargas was abandoning economic liberalism and adopting import substitution policies (Dean, 1969:207-33). In 1937 a Department of
Agricultural and Industrial Credit was created in the Bank of Brazil, and import permits were initiated with a scale of priorities
emphasizing machinery and transportation equipment over consumer
goods. The "Law of Similars" was used to protect some industrial
products, though administration was lax and often delayed (Leff,
1968:12). The most important act signifying the government's commitment to industrialization was the 1939 announcement that the
government, aided by domestic entrepreneurs, would build the nation's first integrated steel mill at Volta Redonda in the state
of Rio de Janeiro.[5] These policies represented a new commitment
not just to import substitution but to the establishment of heavy
industries.

Deliberate protectionism began in 1947 with the establishment
of import controls through licensing.[6] Protectionism increased
around 1949 when the state, under the authority of the "Law of
Similars," began prohibiting the importation of products for which
domestic substitutes existed. In 1953 control by licensing was
replaced by a five category exchange auction system (multiple exchange rates). The degree and structure of protectionism changed
little throughout the licensing and auction periods. In August of
1957 the emphasis of protectionism switched from exchange control
to tariff revision. The exchange system was simplified as the five
rates were reduced to two, while a new tariff law (Law 3244) replaced the specific tariff, which lost its effectiveness due to
inflation, with an ad valorem tariff. Baer (1965:57) describes
this new tariff law as an expansion and solidification of protectionism for the growing industrial sector. By 1961 all imports had
been transferred to the free market rate of exchange, so that the
tariff and the prohibition of imports through the "Law of Similars"
were the sole instruments of protectionist policy. In 1967 tariffs
were revised downward, but data on net import protection from 1954
to 1967 indicate that the level of protection began to decrease in
1964 (Bergsman and Malan, 1971:116).

Other forms of state promotion of industry also became important

Figure 3.2

Summary of Brazilian Industrialization Policies, 1930-64

Date	Policy	Emphasis
1930	exchange control	consumer goods
	tariffs	consumer goods
1937	Department of Agricultural and Industrial Credit (credit expansion)	consumer goods
	import permits	capital goods
1939-46	Volta Redonda steel mill (public investment)	capital goods
1947	import licensing	consumer and capital goods
1949	"Law of Similars" (import prohibition)	consumer and capital goods
1952	BNDE (credit expansion)	consumer and capital goods
1953	multiple exchange rates	consumer and capital goods
1954	Petrobrás (public investment)	capital goods
1956-60	public investment	capital goods
1957	ad valorem tariff	consumer and capital goods
1961-64	protection de-emphasized	

in the postwar period (Bergsman and Candal, 1969:30-36). The state-owned steel mill at Volta Redonda began production in 1946, the National Economic Development Bank (BNDE) was created in 1952 to analyze and finance various development projects, and the state-owned petroleum monopoly, Petrobrás, was founded in 1954. The greatest increase in public investment and mixed enterprises was under the presidency of Kubitschek (1956-60), when the public sector's share of the GDP grew from 26.8 percent in 1956 to 38.3 percent in 1962 (Gudin, 1969:20).

The commitment to heavy industries in Brazil has been much stronger than in Argentina and came earlier relative to the beginning of significant industrialization.[7] Policies to promote heavy industries became important around 1947, as the protectionism afforded by the postwar policies was much more diversified in terms of product categories than that before the War. Actually, the government had demonstrated its commitment to basic industries even earlier when it constructed the Volta Redonda steel works in the early forties. Though the highest rates of protection were still granted to consumer goods industries after 1947, producer goods industries were promoted through public investment, low-interest loans, and special treatment in importing necessary inputs.

Chile

Protectionist policies in Chile were first initiated in the early 1930s as a response to balance of payments difficulties, and deliberate industrialization policies began in 1938.[8] These deliberate policies of industrial promotion more directly involved sectoral clash than those in Argentina, where the policies of agro-export discrimination were a more important component of sectoral clash than those of industrial promotion. The Chilean protectionist and investment policies after the late 1930s were a significant cause of the neglect of the agricultural sector and the suppression of the mining-export sector.

Protectionist policies in Chile actually began with the new tariff law (Law 4321) in 1928 which provided for specific duties on imports, increased a wide range of duties, and gave the President the power to raise any duty 35 percent.[9] Other policies in the late

1920s that stimulated industry included the development of credit
agencies and vast public works programs.[10] From 1930 to 1932 a host
of policies was initiated that was intended as a temporary response
to the balance of payments deficits Chile experienced after the Depression. Tariffs were increased from 1930 to 1932, exchange control was introduced in 1931, and import licenses and quotas were
created in 1932 (Ellsworth, 1945:49-51; Inter-American Development
Commission, 1946:46, 164). These policies were applied in a general
and non-discriminatory manner and were designed primarily as emergency measures to alleviate the immediate crisis caused by the Depression, though an additional outcome of exchange control was the
extraction of resources from the copper companies. Not until the
late 1930s did policies begin to deliberately encourage specific
industries in a systematic way.

The election of the Popular Front government in 1938 brought
to power for the first time in Chile a regime that was publicly
committed to industrial promotion.[11] Not only were protectionist
policies intensified and more directly related to the encouragement
of certain industries, but public investment, subsidies, tax exemptions, and low-cost credits were used to promote industrial
growth. The most important accomplishment of the Popular Front
in this area was the creation of the Chilean Development Corporation (CORFO) in 1939, which planned and directed the industrial
promotion effort.[12] Since its inception, CORFO has played a central role in the Chilean economy. It has controlled much of the
total investment in machinery and equipment (30 percent in 1939-54),
more than one-quarter of total public investment, and as much as
18 percent (in 1954) of the GDP (Mamalakis, 1969b:118). The creation of CORFO, which was financed by the additional tax on the copper companies, is the best example of the correspondence between
sectoral clash and industrialization policies in Chile.

Another important measure was the creation by executive decree
in 1942 (Law No. 14/164) of the National Foreign Trade Council
(Consejo Nacional de Comercio Exterior), which absorbed the International Exchange Commission, the Export Control Service, the Import License Commission, and the National Supply Board.[13] Due to

Figure 3.3

Summary of Chilean Industrialization Policies, 1928-55

Date	Policy	Emphasis
1928-30	tariff law	consumer goods
	credit agencies	consumer goods
	public investment	capital goods
1930-32	tariff increase	consumer goods
	exchange control	consumer goods
	import licenses and quotas	consumer goods
1938-40	CORFO (public credit and investment)	capital goods
	tax exemptions	consumer goods
1942	National Foreign Trade Council (import restriction)	consumer goods
1943	tax exemptions	consumer goods
1950-55	CAP and other public work projects (public investment)	capital goods
1955	protection de-emphasized	

wartime shortages of imports, especially industrial raw materials, this Council could restrict or prohibit, in accordance with national interest, the importation of superfluous goods or goods that could be produced domestically. Also, in an effort to encourage new industries, Law No. 7747 (December 1943) exempted from the excess profits tax for a period of ten years those industrial firms established after January 1, 1942 (Inter-American Development Commission, 1946:47). All of these policies remained intact until 1955 when a number of exchange liberalization and stabilization policies were enacted (Jeanneret, 1971:147-52).

Although protectionist policies have invariably favored consumer goods,[14] in the early 1950s the government did demonstrate a commitment to the development of basic industries. This commitment was carried out primarily through the investment and credit policies of CORFO.[15] In 1950 the government-created steel plant at Huachipato (CAP, or Compañía de Acero del Pacífico) began producing almost all of Chile's steel[16]; in 1954 the important petroleum refinery at Concon became operative; and also in the early fifties there was further electrification of the country through the National Electrification Company. In each of these projects, as well as others in metal processing, electrical goods, and chemicals, CORFO was a major participant.

Mexico

Despite earlier measures granting some tax exemptions to new industries, expanding public credit institutions, and increasing tariffs for some industries, economic policies were not deliberately used to protect and promote industry until after 1940.[17] Promotion of industry through tax exemptions and credit policies became important in 1939-41 while foreign trade policies became deliberately protectionist in 1944-47.

Tax exemptions have been an important part of industrial promotion law in Mexico. A 1939 decree and the 1941 Law of Manufacturing Industries granted five-year exemptions from virtually all federal taxes to "new and necessary" industries.[18] The 1946 Law for the Development of Manufacturing Industries extended exemptions to more industries and granted exemptions for up to ten years, though

eligibility requirements became more precise and fewer taxes were
covered. Due to changes in the administration of this law in 1948,
even fewer taxes were exempted, and restrictions were applied to the
qualifying firms, such as requiring a certain amount of inputs to
be bought in Mexico and fixing price ceilings. The Law for the Development of New and Necessary Industries in 1955 codified these
restrictions. Though the number of qualified firms and the amount
of the exemptions were being reduced, the government was furthering
its effort to promote import substitution and industrial integration (see note 18 here).

Public credit and investment became significant factors in
industrial development in December 1940 when a new charter reorgan-
ized the national development bank, Nacional Financiera (NAFIN), to
concentrate on industrial development.[19] From then until 1946-47,
NAFIN's principal assets were in iron and steel, electrical appli-
ances, sugar, paper, and fertilizers. One of its most notable ac-
complishments was the Altos Hornos de México iron and steel plant
at Monclava in the northern state of Coahuila. This project was
initiated by private capital during the Second World War, but by
1947 NAFIN was the majority stockholder. After 1947 NAFIN's pro-
motional efforts became particularly concentrated in infrastructure
and heavy industry. NAFIN has reflected Mexico's commitment to
import substitution, since a major criterion for assistance has
been the potential for import replacement (Blair, 1964:225-26).

Protectionist policies have been more important in achieving
industrial growth in Mexico than the credit or tax exemption policies, and the quantitative control of imports through a licensing
system as well as ad valorem tariffs have been the mainstays of
this protectionist system since 1947. Before 1947 the only instrument for protecting domestic industries from foreign competition
was the specific tariff, used mostly for purposes of revenue. In
1930 trade duties and tariffs represented 37 percent of total federal revenues, and in 1940 they were still 23 percent (De la Peña,
1945:190). Some tariffs were high enough to be considered protective in the 1930s (mostly for textile and food products; see Mosk,
1950:68), but in general even the tariff increases were implemented

to raise revenues.[20] The fact that the tariff was assigned according to weight or volume (a specific tariff) was also a detriment
to its having protectionist purposes, since the effect of the tariff
was reduced as the price of imported goods increased. Finally, in
December 1942 the United States and Mexico signed a trade agreement
in which both countries agreed not to increase certain tariff rates
(Mosk, 1950:72; and Izquierdo, 1964:251-52, 264-65). This further
inhibited any attempts to increase the protectionist nature of
Mexican tariffs.

The protectionist era in Mexican trade policy was ushered in
by two dramatic decrees in July 1947: the creation of import controls and a change in the tariff system.[21] The official purpose
of these measures was to correct the balance of payments deficits
incurred after World War II, but the actual effect was protection
from foreign competition for many Mexican industries. The tariff
decree increased a number of duties, and in November 1947 the method
of levying duties was changed from specific to compound (a combination of specific and ad valorem methods), which halted the erosion
of the effectiveness of the specific rate. Most of the items se-
lected for the tariff increases, which were as much as 100-200 percent, were essential consumer goods, strongly suggesting a protectionist purpose behind the new tariffs (Mosk, 1950:75).

The import control system had actually been created in 1944
under an emergency war powers act, but it was not applied until
1947. The type of goods subjected to import licensing under the
1944 decree suggests that an underlying purpose was protectionism
for import-substituting industries. Up to the summer of 1947 the
government had one general list and several minor lists of goods
requiring permits, and the majority of these goods were semi-manu-
factured or finished products that were competing with domestic
output (Mosk, 1950:80-81; and Strassman, 1968:289). The controls
were not applied, however, until July 1947, when a group of luxury
goods representing some 18 percent of total imports in 1946 were
prevented from entering Mexico in order to correct the balance of
payments deficit. Yet even this ban on luxury goods was adopted
with an eye to protectionism. For instance, the ban on automobiles

Figure 3.4

Summary of Mexican Industrialization Policies, 1916-64

Date	Policy	Emphasis
1916	tariff increases	consumer goods
1920	tax exemptions	consumer goods
1926	tax exemptions	consumer goods
1930	tariff law	consumer goods
1932	tax exemptions	consumer goods
1933-40	NAFIN (public credit and investment)	consumer and capital goods
	public works	capital goods
	Industrial Development Bank (credit expansion)	consumer goods
1939	tax exemptions	consumer goods
1940	NAFIN reorganized (public credit and investment)	consumer and capital goods
1941	Law of Manufacturing Industries (tax exemptions)	consumer goods
1944	import controls	consumer goods
1946	Law for the Development of Manufacturing Industries (tax exemptions)	consumer and capital goods
1947	Altos Hornos de México steel mill (public investment)	capital goods
	import controls	consumer and capital goods
	tariff increases and ad valorem tariff	consumer goods
1954	import controls extended	consumer goods
1955	Law for the Development of New and Necessary Industries (tax exemptions)	consumer and capital goods
1959	import controls	consumer and capital goods
1964	protection de-emphasized	

was accompanied by annual quotas on imports of assembly parts, so
that between 1946 and 1948 the number of automobiles assembled in
Mexico increased from 10,460 to 21,597 (Izquierdo, 1964:265).

Thus, the 1944 decree and the 1947 application of import controls, along with the 1947 changes in the tariff system, set up the
framework for the protectionist system of postwar Mexico. The import controls were eased in 1951 but reimposed and extended in 1954
when a number of consumer goods were added to the list of controlled
imports. Beginning in 1959, industrial integration was emphasized
as a major objective of protectionist policies (Izquierdo, 1964:
273; and King, 1970:42), though by 1964 protectionism seemed to have
passed its peak with more emphasis being placed on manufactured exports and efficient production (Strassman, 1968:290-91; and Bueno,
1971:199-202).

Venezuela

Industrialization policies were not stressed until the mid-
1940s, though even before World War I, Venezuela had relatively
high import duties, mostly for revenue purposes.[22] The only other
efforts by the government to promote industrial growth before 1943
were the creation of the Banco Industrial de Venezuela in 1937 and
legislation enacted in 1938 and 1939 to encourage new industries
by authorizing the executive to grant exemptions from import duties
on necessary equipment for new industries (Wythe, 1949:267-68).
Modern protectionist policies were not initiated until 1943 and
1944 when exchange control began.[23] A 1945 decree placed certain
imports on a yearly quota (Loreto and Lepervanche Parpercen, 1949:
164-65), and in the same year import duties were raised to encourage domestic industrialization (Feinstein, 1965:197). The most
significant policy initiative in this period was the creation of
the Venezuelan Development Corporation (Corporación Venezolana de
Fomento, or CVF) in 1946 as a semi-autonomous body to promote economic development.[24] The Development Corporation's principal functions have been to extend credit to agricultural and industrial
entrepreneurs,[25] to aid in establishing government enterprises in
key industries, and to provide government technical assistance to
the private sector.

Figure 3.5

Summary of Venezuelan Industrialization Policies, 1937-77

Date	Policy	Emphasis
1937	Industrial Bank (credit expansion)	consumer goods
1938-39	tax exemptions	consumer goods
1943-44	exchange control	consumer goods
1945	import quotas	consumer goods
	tariff increases	consumer goods
	CVF (public credit and investment)	consumer and capital goods
1958	ad valorem tariffs	consumer goods
	import licenses	consumer goods
	expansion of public credit and investment	consumer and capital goods
1960-61	multiple exchange rates	consumer goods

The period of intensive and deliberate protection and promotion of industries began in 1958 (R. Alexander, 1964:194-218; and J.A. Gil, 1977:146). Import duties were thereafter based on ad valorem rates rather than on weight (Feinstein, 1965:209-10), and an import licensing system was used to restrict the importation of goods produced domestically (International Bank for Reconstruction and Development, 1961:205). In 1960 and 1961 multiple exchange rates were instituted which created a devalued exchange rate for non-essential imports.[26] Also, in 1958 the government began making considerably greater amounts of capital available to private manufacturing enterprises through the CVF. From its inception in 1946 to December 1957 the CVF had disbursed some 74 million bolivares to the private sector, but between March 1958 and November 1959 loans totaling 154 million bolivares were granted by the CVF to private enterprises (International Bank for Reconstruction and Development, 1961:215).

Conclusion

The pattern in each country is generally consistent with the expectation that autonomously initiated sectoral clash is more likely to precede the major period of industrialization policies and that state-initiated sectoral clash is more likely to coincide with the major period of industrialization policies. The timing of the most intense periods of sectoral clash and industrialization policies is shown in Table 3.6. In Argentina, Chile, and Venezuela these coincided almost perfectly. To varying degrees, in each of these countries pro-industry policies were in fact an important aspect of sectoral clash: (1) Chilean policies that increased the tax burden on the export sector were used to benefit the industrial sector; (2) the Venezuelan state also employed a large state share of export income to benefit industry, through the state has tried to promote agricultural development as well; and (3) Argentine sectoral clash was primarily a result of policies discriminating against agriculture with industrialization policies being somewhat more peripheral. On the other hand, Mexico and Brazil experienced much earlier sectoral clash, which diminished greatly in importance around 1940 as the industrial sector became dominant. Only then did deliberate industrialization policies begin, and these were not so much instruments of state-initiated sectoral clash as they were attempts to achieve balanced growth with industry as the leading sector. The major exception to this was the overvaluation in Brazil that depressed the export sector from 1945 to 1961.

Also confirmed is the expectation that autonomously initiated sectoral clash is more likely to contribute to policies stressing integrated and diversified industrial growth (backward-linking import substitution) and that state-initiated sectoral clash is less likely to contribute to such policies. In cases in which industrialization policies were part of a state program to reallocate resources among sectors—as in Argentina, Chile, and, to a lesser degree, Venezuela—these policies tended not to emphasize integrated growth. In its attempt to artificially establish the dominance of industry, the state concentrated its efforts on certain segments of industry, especially non-durable consumer goods. However, in Brazil

Figure 3.6

Major Periods of Sectoral Clash and Industrialization Policies

	1910	1920	1930	1940	1950	1960	1970
Argentina							
Sectoral clash					1946–55		
Industrial policies				·1944–53			
Chile							
Sectoral clash				1939–71			
Industrial policies				1938–55			
Venezuela							
Sectoral clash						1958–76	
Industrial policies						1958–77	
Mexico							
Sectoral clash	1910–40						
Industrial policies					1946–64		
Brazil							
Sectoral clash		1920–40					
Industrial policies				1947–64			

and Mexico, where industrialization policies were not an aspect of sectoral clash, policies did emphasize industrial integration.

Industrialization policies in Argentina have probably played the least important role of all five countries in terms of emphasizing and contributing to diversified industrial growth. After an upsurge in the early 1930s, protectionism was reduced for the rest of the decade. When pro-industry policies did become significant in the 1940s, they were oriented more toward benefiting the military and the working class. Despite the advanced stage the industrial sector had reached in the mid-1940s, policies stressed either consumer goods or military-related industries. An abnormally high profit rate was artificially maintained in these industries, which further encouraged speculative investment to concentrate in these areas (Polit, 1968:404-11). Incentives were not to improve efficiency, so labor productivity decreased, thereby contributing to inflation. Díaz Alejandro (1970:106-26) says that these policies were at least ill-timed and suggests that the emphasis in the immediate postwar period should have been on those industries "at the frontier of import substitution," i.e., oil extraction and refining, steel, machinery, and chemicals. Only after 1953 was a commitment made to develop these basic industries.

Chilean industrialization policies in the 1930s were emphasized more than those in Argentina, but as in Argentina the emphasis was on consumer goods even through the 1950s. Data for 1961 show that the highest levels of protection were for food products, beverages, tobacco, and other non-durable consumer goods (Jeanneret, 1971:156, 161). Yet in the early 1950s the government, primarily through CORFO, began to promote some development in basic industries.

More so than in Argentina or Chile, Venezuelan industrialization policies have been aimed at those areas with the most potential for import substitution, though these policies have been less influential than petroleum policies in terms of affecting either industrial or overall economic growth. In the 1950s industrial growth progressed not because of government promotion or protection but rather because of the expansion of petroleum production.[27] Only after 1958 did government policies for protection, technical and financial aid, tax incentives, and investment begin to aid industrial development (Machado Gómez, 1968:22). Since 1958 there have been large public investments in iron and steel, petrochemicals, ship repairing and maintenance, aluminum, and oil refining (International Bank for Reconstruction and Development, 1961:221-35; and R. Alexander, 1964:206-18). There have also been attempts to favor modern industries such as automotive assembly and pharmaceuticals through greater protection (R. Alexander, 1964:197; and Blank, 1971:95-98), though the highest protectionist rates still apply to consumer goods industries such as foodstuffs, leather, textiles, and tobacco products (International Bank for Reconstruction and Development, 1961:204-07).

Brazilian and Mexican industrialization policies have been the most consistently committed to modernization, integration, and diversification. These countries have encouraged a larger degree of import substitution in sectors other than consumer non-durables at earlier time periods than the other countries. One of the best distinctions in terms of the different emphases of industrialization policies is the contrast between the Argentine industrial promotion law of 1944 that stressed national defense industries and the Mexican industrial promotion law of 1941 that stressed import-substituting industries (see note 18 here). The 1941 Mexican law was the earliest industrial promotion law that specifically stated import substitution as a goal. Another important distinction is that both Mexico and Brazil established government-owned iron and steel plants in the 1940s, which was earlier than in the other countries.

Postwar policies in Mexico and Brazil clearly emphasized backward-linking import substitution.[28] Consumer durable goods were stimulated by the Mexican protectionist policies of the late 1940s, with the import ban on previously assembled automobiles being a prime example (King, 1970:33). Then in the late 1950s, the government began stressing integration in basic industries like automobiles and electronics, and required 60 percent of the cost of automobiles to be furnished domestically (Izquierdo,

1964:273; and King, 1970:42). Postwar industrialization policies
in Brazil were designed to maximize vertical integration in industry by promoting a wide array of intermediate and capital goods industries as well as consumer goods industries. For example, government promotion of the automobile industry began in 1952 when
imports of automobile parts that were also produced domestically
were banned (Bergsman, 1970:125).

Notes

[1]These are usually followed by a period when protectionism is de-emphasized in favor of efficiency.

[2]Wythe (1949:84), Chu (1972:14-16, 21), and Goldwert (1972: 36-37).

[3]Murmis and Portantiero (1971:10-13). As further evidence of the lack of conflict between agriculture and industry in the 1930s, Gustavo Polit (1968:412) quotes two leading industrial spokesmen in 1933 as proclaiming that there could never be any conflicting interests between industrial and agrarian activities.

[4]On post-1953 developments in economic policy, see Mallon (1968), Díaz Alejandro (1970:254-71), and Mallon and Sourrouille (1975:14-34).

[5]Probably the group most directly responsible for building the Volta Redonda plant was the military. The armed forces felt that basic industries were needed to make Brazil a powerful nation with adequate military security. The interest of the army in this specific enterprise is shown by the fact that the construction of Volta Redonda was managed by an army officer, Edmundo de Macedo Soares, who also served as its first director. See Leff (1968:48), Dean (1969:212, 217, 219), and Schmitter (1971:309).

[6]For detailed descriptions of protectionist policies in Brazil after 1947, see Baer (1965:48-77), Bergsman (1970:27-54), and Bergsman and Malan (1971).

[7]On government promotion of capital goods as well as consumer goods industries, see UNECLA (1964:160-70), Baer (1965:65-68), Leff (1968:43), Bergsman (1970:96-97, 105-10, 125-27), Morley and Smith (1971:121), Baer and Villela (1973:230), and Cardoso (1976: 143).

[8]Mamalakis (1965:15-18), Muñoz (1971:79), and Jeanneret (1971: 143-46).

[9]This law took effect before the balance of payments diffi-culties began in 1931, and it is the only example in Chile of a policy that was not primarily state-initiated but rather was, to a great extent, a response to demands from industrialists. How-ever, the degree to which entrepreneurs could act autonomously to affect economic policy even in the late 1920s is in question. In these years the government established a series of official boards and corporate bodies designed to promote and control the principal aspects of Chilean economic life: an agricultural bank (Caja de Crédito Agrario), a rural colonization bank (Caja de Colonización Agrario), a mining bank (Caja de Crédito Minero), an industrial credit bank (Instituto de Crédito Industrial), and a foreign com-merce institute (Instituto de Comercio Exterior). See Ellsworth

(1945:95) and Wythe (1949:219-20). Also, Burnett (1970:146) maintains that in the 1920s the landed oligarchy retained political dominance while making certain accommodations to the emerging industrial and commercial elites. The 1928 tariff law could be interpreted as part of this accommodation.

[10]See J. Johnson (1965:79-90), Nunn (1970:148-50), and Strawbridge (1971:31-32). The credit agencies are listed in note 9.

[11]A principal plank of the platform of the Popular Front presidential candidate in 1938, Pedro Aguirre Cerda, was the need for industrialization in order to raise the Chilean standard of living (UNECLA, 1967:4).

[12]John Reese Stevenson (1942:123-24) concludes that "it is in its efforts to assist Chilean industry and raise the level of production that the Popular Front realized its most singular administrative success. Even most Rightists admit that the Development Corporation, the governmental agency set up for this purpose, has been remarkably successful." See also UNECLA (1967:107-08) and Soza (1968:618-21).

[13]Ellsworth (1945:78) says that "this decree was based on the Emergency Powers Act (Law 7200) of July 21, 1942, which among other things authorized the executive to undertake a thorough reorganization of the civil functions of the government." On the National Foreign Trade Council, also see Ellsworth (1945:58-59) and the Inter-American Development Commission (1946:165-66).

[14]For example, in 1961 a great majority of the items with prohibitive tariffs was concentrated in non-durable consumer goods (Jeanneret, 1971:156,161).

[15]On CORFO's promotion of basic industries, see Leiserson (1966:46-47), UNECLA (1967:5-6), Soza (1968:618-21), Mamalakis (1969b), and Cavarozzi (1975:263-70).

[16]The construction of CAP began in 1946 aided by a loan from the Export-Import Bank.

[17]The 1916 tariff increase and the 1920 tax exemptions were mentioned in Chapter 2. Tax exemptions for some industries were also decreed in 1927 and 1932, though these had little effect until they were extended considerably around 1940 (Ross and Christensen, 1959:42-43, 187-89; Glade, 1963:85; and King, 1970:99). In the 1930s the expansion of public credit institutions and the inflationary financing of public works were somewhat beneficial to industry (Glade, 1955:76-78; and 1963:19-20, 45; Vernon, 1963:72; Shelton, 1964:141-46; Aubey, 1966:23-38; Labastida Martín del Campo, 1972:105-08; and Hansen,1974:49). Nacional Financiera was created in December 1933 to engage in a wide variety of financial operations including making industrial loans (Blair, 1964:206-11; and Aubey, 1966:36-38). Also, in 1937 the Industrial Development Bank (Banco Nacional Obrero y de Fomento Industrial) was created

(C. Anderson, 1963:123; and Aubey, 1966:23). The 1930 tariff law, which placed the highest levies of 40-100 percent on textiles, was the basis for all future tariff legislation, but in the 1930s tariffs were still primarily for revenue purposes (Mosk, 1950:68; King, 1970:10; and Reynolds, 1970:216-18).

[18]The differences between the Argentine and Mexican industrialization policies in the 1940s are shown by contrasting the interpretation of "necessary" industries contained in the Argentine industrial promotion law of 1944 and the Mexican 1941 Law of Manufacturing Industries. The Argentine law granted subsidies to "industries of importance from the standpoint of national defense" (Wythe, 1949:126), while the Mexican law granted tax exemptions to those industries "which are devoted to the manufacture or preparation of goods not produced in the country in sufficient quantity to meet the needs of domestic consumption" (Bernal-Molina, 1948:81). Thus, the Argentine law was more to the benefit of the military, and the Mexican law was clearly designed as a boost to import-substituting industries. For more detail on the 1939 decree and the 1941, 1946, and 1955 laws in Mexico, see Mosk (1950: 64-66), Bernal-Molina (1956:93-95), Ross and Christensen (1959: 43-54, 191-240), Glade (1963:85), Strassman (1968:297-98), and King (1970:99-106).

[19]On the history, purpose, and effect of NAFIN, see Bernal-Molina (1948:160-61), Ross and Christensen (1959:34-38), C. Anderson (1963:124-25), Blair (1964), Brandenburg (1964:71-72), Aubey (1966:38-52), LaCascia (1969:39-42), and King (1970:71-74).

[20]The average tariff rate was only 16 percent _ad valorem_, which is hardly a protectionist tariff (Reynolds, 1970:216-18). Also see Mosk (1950:68-69).

[21]On these 1947 decrees, see Mosk (1950:74-83), Ross and Christensen (1959:29-32), Izquierdo (1964:263-66), Strassman (1968:288-89), King (1970:32-33, 75-76), and Bueno (1971:180-82).

[22]George Wythe (1949:264) quotes authors who describe Venezuelan duties before World War I as "enormous" and "higher than in any other country in South America," and he says that in 1940 investigators found Venezuelan import duties to be about the highest in the world. On the history of high import duties in Venezuela, also see the International Bank for Reconstruction and Development (1961:204-07).

[23]The beneficial petroleum exchange rate was ended and special exchange rates were instituted for coffee and cacao exports (Feinstein, 1965:192). The two existing selling rates for importers were stabilized at 3.35 bolivares/dollar (International Monetary Fund, _International Financial Statistics 1948_). Also see Loreto and Lepervanche Parparcen (1949:164-65).

[24]Loreto and Lepervanche Parparcen (1949:161-63), Wythe (1949:

268), International Bank for Reconstruction and Development (1961: 215-41), and Brandenburg (1964:72-73).

[25]According to David E. Blank (1973:40), since 1958 the CVF has concentrated its investment activities in the industrial sector, and government credit to agriculture has shifted to the Agricultural and Livestock Bank (Banco Agricola y Pecuaria, or BAP). On the credit policies of the Development Corporation and the Industrial Bank, also see Falcón Urbano (1969:194-200).

[26]International Monetary Fund, International Financial Statistics 1961; Falcón Urbano (1969:193); and Harris (1971:146).

[27]Robert Alexander (1964:194-95) says that industrial growth occurred in the 1950s in spite of the actions of the Pérez Jiménez regime. Also, the International Bank for Reconstruction and Development (1961:196) says that in the 1950s ineffective tariff protection caused slower growth in industries such as tobacco products and cotton textiles.

[28]Macario (1964:65-66) emphasizes that in contrast to most other Latin American countries, industrialization policies in Brazil and Mexico in the late 1950s were aimed at achieving industrial integration in the import substitution process.

Chapter 4

CONCLUSION

The final objective of this monograph is to relate these differences in type of sectoral clash and industrialization policies
to achievements in industrial growth and to crucial changes in political regimes. Particularly through its promotion of policies of
industrial integration, autonomously initiated sectoral clash can
be expected to contribute to more successful aggregate industrial
growth, while state-initiated sectoral clash that is part of a state
program of sectoral discrimination is more likely to produce slower
industrial growth. In the political realm, these patterns of sectoral clash can be linked to aspects of political change surrounding
populist and bureaucratic-authoritarian regimes.

Sectoral Clash and Industrial Growth

As expected, qualitative comparisons of countries confirm the
relation between types of sectoral clash, industrialization policies, and industrial growth. The countries which experienced state-
initiated sectoral clash and in which industrialization policies did
not emphasize balance and backward-linking industrialization (Argentina and Chile) also have had the lowest levels of industrial growth
(see Table 4.1). Those countries in which sectoral clash was initiated autonomously of the state and in which industrialization
policies stressed integrated industrial expansion (Brazil and Mexico)
have had much higher levels of industrial growth (Table 4.1). The
only anomaly is Venezuela, which was an intermediate case in terms
of the type of sectoral clash and the emphasis of industrialization
policies, but which has had the most rapid industrial growth (Table
4.1).

The influence of the type of sectoral clash on industrial
growth is evident through differences in the timing of the clash and
its impact on policies. In cases of state-initiated sectoral clash,

71

Table 4.1

Average Annual Disaggregate Growth Rates in Industry*

(percentages)

	Argentina (1900-74)	Brazil (1920-75)	Chile (1914-75)	Mexico (1929-75)	Venezuela (1936-75)
Consumer Goods	3.8	5.7	2.8	5.5	7.8
Intermediate Goods	6.1	9.8	4.5	9.4	11.2
Capital Goods	7.5	9.1	6.3	10.7	13.4
TOTAL	5.3	7.3	3.5	7.6	9.3

*These data have been collected from a wide variety of UN and government sources using the following criteria for selecting the best data: (1) use of disaggregate price indices to deflate current values; (2) use of a "base year" for valuing output that does not have any disproportionately high prices in any industrial category; and (3) use of the most comparable data available.

such as Argentina and Chile, the clash began much later than in cases of autonomously initiated clash. Sectoral clash did not begin until the 1940s in these countries. Despite the severe damage to the export sector done by the Depression in 1930, the traditional export elite in Argentina and Chile continued to dominate in the 1930s and to allow only limited industrialization. Industrialization was designed only as a temporary response to external payments problems and was no threat to agricultural dominance. The state eventually initiated the clash between the industrial sector and the export sector around the 1940s (1946 in Argentina and 1939 in Chile), but this still did not serve to stimulate industry, especially the dynamic or heavy industrial sectors.

One of the reasons that the initiation of sectoral clash in Argentina and Chile had no positive influence on industrial growth is that industrialization policies were more an integral part of a strategy of sectoral discrimination than an instrument of industrial

promotion. State-initiated sectoral clash appeared late and coincided with the establishment of significant industrialization policies. The large role of the state in favoring industry over other
sectors resulted in a greater chance for the misallocation of resources. The state, in its attempt to transfer resources to industry, tended to apply political rather than economic criteria in
allocating resources within industry.

Argentine industrialization policies in the 1940s were primarily directed against the agricultural sector, which was probably
the foremost political opponent of the Peronist government, and in
favor of the military and labor, which were the backbone of Peronist
support. Chilean economic policies in the 1940s followed a similar
pattern: income was transferred from the export sector to labor-
intensive, consumer goods industries. In both countries, there was
no appreciable attempt to stimulate backward-linking industrialization until the 1950s, well after the time the transition from
light to heavy industries should have been promoted. Thus, even
in recent decades industrial growth in Argentina and Chile has been
much slower than that of the other three nations.

Venezuela is a unique case in which sectoral clash in some
ways has approximated the pattern described for Argentina and Chile
(late and largely state-initiated) but in which industrial growth
has surpassed that in even Brazil and Mexico. The major explana-
tory factor for this situation has been the dominance and the importance of the petroleum sector. The emergence of petroleum as
the principal export product in the 1920s as well as the agricultural background of the Venezuelan political elite up to the 1940s
delayed the beginning of significant industrialization. At least
until the 1940s, there was no industrial sector capable of challenging the export sector; the importance of the petroleum sector
and its foreign ownership required the state to take the initiative in the clash with the export sector. The industrialists continued to be subordinate to other economic groups for several
decades after 1940. Yet industrial growth has been the most rapid
of all five countries, and the wealth of the petroleum sector has
been an important factor. At least up to the present, the petroleum

sector has been sufficiently prosperous to allow for the distribution of substantial income from petroleum to industry and other
sectors without adversely affecting the vitality of petroleum exports.

In contrast to the cases of state-initiated sectoral clash,
autonomously initiated clash occurred much earlier in Brazil and
Mexico. Brazilian industrialists successfully challenged the export and commercial elites in the 1920s and 1930s for both economic
and political power. Sectoral clash began in Mexico in the 1910s,
and Mexican industry had consolidated its dominant position by the
1940s.

Growth in the intermediate and capital goods industries in
Brazil and Mexico occurred relatively early, partly as a result of
an early state commitment to these branches of industry. Autonomously initiated sectoral clash preceded the establishment of major
industrialization policies, and the role of the state in favoring
industry over other sectors was less important than in Argentina
and Chile. Since industrialization policies were not a part of a
state strategy of sectoral discrimination, they could more ration-
ally focus on industrial promotion along with balanced growth. The
state was able to encourage new areas of industrial growth in the
intermediate and capital goods sectors.

Partly due to the policies that emphasized integrated industrial growth and partly due to the emerging dominance of the industrial sector, growth in the dynamic industries in Brazil and Mexico
climbed to over 10 percent annually as early as 1935. Industrial
growth rates in these and other industries have remained at relatively high levels throughout the postwar period. Thus, autonomously initiated sectoral clash contributed to successful industrialization policies that promoted integrated and backward-linking
industrial growth.

Sectoral Clash and Political Change

As was mentioned in the Introduction, one of the earliest ap-
plications of a theory of sectoral clash to Latin America emphasized
the influence of sectoral conflict on the transition from a "traditional, government-export sector coalition" to a "modern,

government-industry coalition" (Mamalakis, 1969a and 1971a). The findings of this research concerning differences in the pattern of sectoral clash among countries further suggest that these factors affect political change in terms of the establishment or breakdown of various regime types.

The most salient regime types in terms of political change in Latin America have been populism and bureaucratic-authoritarianism. Populist regimes are those which first incorporate into the ruling coalition both organized labor and national industrial entrepreneurs. These usually are said to follow a period of "hegemonic crisis" within the traditional oligarchy in which the agro-export elite finds its economic and political base threatened (Nun, 1969). A populist regime then emerges and promotes import-substituting industrialization. This coalition temporarily enjoys positive trade balances, large foreign exchange reserves, and the prosperity of initial import substitution that is relatively easy to achieve.

However, as some theorists have claimed, this economic boom reaches its end when the "easy" phase of import substitution in consumer goods is exhausted and the small, inefficient domestic producers cannot serve as the base from which the economy can "take off." The nation begins to face the problems of large imports of intermediate and capital goods, trade imbalances, foreign exchange shortages, and inflation. These economic problems create a political environment conducive to the establishment of bureaucratic-authoritarian regimes in which the military along with economic technocrats acquire dominant political status. The emphasis is on promoting advanced industrialization, favoring transnational corporations, and repressing the lower classes. Thus, the industrialists and the urban proletariat relinquish power to military rulers in conjunction with domestic bureaucrats and foreign entrepreneurs.

The differences in the patterns of sectoral clash, particularly the timing of the clash, can be shown to have had an impact on some of these aspects of political change in the five nations of this study. Generally, early sectoral clash led to populism that stressed the support of domestic industrialists (and hence more successful industrial growth) and to relatively stable bureaucratic-authoritarian governments, while later sectoral clash contributed to populism that relied more on labor support (and less successful industrial growth) and, at least in the case of Argentina, to more unstable bureaucratic-authoritarianism.

The initiation of sectoral clash in Brazil and Mexico preceded both the onset of import substitution and the emergence of populism. The industrial sector successfully displaced the agro-export sector as the dominant economic force by 1940, especially in Mexico. Sectoral clash in these two countries ended the threat that dominance by the agro-export elites posed to industrialization. This also affected populism by making the support of labor and peasants less crucial, because industrial elites depend less on lower-class support when sectoral conflict is minimal. Since populism in Brazil and Mexico was not plagued with sectoral antagonisms, it did not have to placate labor demands to as great an extent as in Argentina and Chile and it was better able to emphasize capital-intensive, heavy industries.

The period in Mexico that has most often been associated with populism was actually short-lived, since it was concentrated in the Cárdenas years from 1934 to 1940; but much of the period after 1940 also had certain populist overtones, especially in that industrialization received top priority from the state and from the private sector. The early sectoral clash during the Revolution did much to destroy the dominance of the traditional oligarchy, and the reforms of the Cárdenas era (nationalizations and agrarian reform) capped the demise of the agro-export elite. These changes contributed to a populist period that was not beset with the struggle for industrial emergence against an entrenched primary products export sector, and in the 1940s Mexico was prepared to begin its prolonged phase of industrial growth tied to political stability.

In Brazil the fall of the agrarian elite was not as swift or as final as in Mexico. The Brazilian populist regime under Vargas (1930-45) probably granted more concessions to labor and even to the agro-export sector than that in Mexico. Indeed, before the creation of the Estado Novo in 1937 the policies of Vargas tended to continue the favoritism toward the coffee planters. However, after

1937 the development strategy shifted to import substitution, and despite the currency overvaluation in the 1950s the principal developmental goal of almost all postwar governments has been industrialization.

Early sectoral clash has also probably aided the more stable transition to bureaucratic-authoritarianism in Brazil and Mexico. Since labor was generally well controlled by the state during the populist period (partly due to early sectoral clash), labor demands in the bureaucratic-authoritarian period have been minimized. Also, as at least one author has argued, the stability and continuity of bureaucratic-authoritarian regimes depends upon the degree to which domestic industrialists are incorporated into the dominant coalition (O'Donnell, 1975:22-41). With the dominance of industry having been established during the populist period in Brazil and Mexico, domestic industrialists either have never left the governing coalition (Mexico) or have maintained influential links to the policy-making apparatus (Brazil). Of course, the bureaucratic-authoritarian period in Mexico is difficult to distinguish. Since 1940, Mexico has had stable, one-party authoritarianism with a heavy industrial orientation and only moderately repressive labor policies; in many ways, this may be the most successful form of "bureaucratic-authoritarianism" (with certain "populist" overtones, as mentioned above).

Sectoral clash in Argentina, Chile, and Venezuela occurred after the onset of ISI and the emergence of populism. This has not had a tremendous effect in Venezuela, where a second populist period began in 1958 backed by extensive petroleum revenues. But in Argentina and Chile, this late sectoral clash has affected import substitution, populism, and bureaucratic-authoritarianism. Since the issue of industrial dominance was not settled and since the threat of the agro-export elite to industrialization was not ended, industrial growth has been much less successful than in Brazil and Mexico.

When many Latin American nations were beginning to move away from export-oriented political regimes in the 1930s, both Argentina and Chile maintained the dominance of the conservative coalition

in the decade following the Depression. The political power of the
agrarian oligarchs was particularly evident in Argentina during the
Justo administration, which favored the export sector with such
policies as the Roca-Runciman Treaty. The lack of any industrial
challenge to the position of the grain and cattle growers did not
change significantly in the 1940s. Perón did transfer resources
out of the agrarian sector using IAPI, but the principal benefac-
tors were urban labor and the military. In the populist periods,
the support of labor in the conflict with the agro-export oligarchy
was actually more crucial than that of industry. Sectoral clash was
initiated by the state, which found that labor was a more important
ally than industrial elites. Perón's base of support came from
labor and the military, and industry was dependent on Perón rather
than vice versa. Though the actual policies of the Popular Front
in Chile did not favor labor as much as its rhetoric claimed, the
state did support a large increase in the number of unionized workers in this period, and, as in Argentina, the industrial elite was
dominated by the state.

Late sectoral clash in Argentina and Chile also has affected
the relatively unsuccessful bureaucratic-authoritarian regimes.
The base that labor built under the populist regimes (partly due to
continued sectoral conflict in the populist period) has made the
repression of labor a difficult task. Also, the weak and dependent
status of industrialists in the populist period has generally continued into the bureaucratic-authoritarian period, in which domestic industrialists have not been a major factor in the dominant
coalition. Hence, bureaucratic-authoritarian regimes in Argentina
since 1966 have not been able to solve the problems of economic
stagnation, inflation, and political instability. The Chilean experience with bureaucratic-authoritarianism has been more recent,
and though it is too early to reach conclusive judgments, we can
note continued reliance on extremely repressive measures and an
economic performance less successful than expected, particularly
in industry.

mutually reinforcing

REFERENCES

This bibliography is divided into six sections: a general references section followed by sections for each of the five Latin American nations in this study.

I. General References

Barraza, Luciano
1969 The Relevance of the Theory of Sectoral Clashes to the Mexican Economy. Latin American Research Review 4(3): 73-87.

Domínguez, Jorge I.
1971 Sectoral Clashes in Cuban Politics and Development. Latin American Research Review 6(3):61-87.

Hirschman, Albert O.
1968 The Political Economy of Import-Substituting Industriali-zation in Latin America. The Quarterly Journal of Economics 82(1):1-32.

Mamalakis, Markos J.
1965 Public Policy and Sectoral Development: A Case Study of Chile, 1940-1958. In Essays on the Chilean Economy. Markos J. Mamalakis and Clark Reynolds. Homewood, Illinois: Irwin Publishers.

1969a The Theory of Sectoral Clashes. Latin American Research Review 4(3):9-46.

1971a The Theory of Sectoral Clashes and Coalitions Revisited. Latin American Research Review 6(3):89-126.

Marx, Karl and Friedrich Engels
1955 The Communist Manifesto. Samuel H. Beer, ed. New York: Appleton-Century-Crofts.

Merkx, Gilbert
1969 Sectoral Clashes and Political Change: The Argentine Experience. Latin American Research Review 4(3):89-114.

Moore, Barrington, Jr.
1966 Social Origins of Dictatorship and Democracy: Lord and Peasant in the Making of the Modern World. Boston: Beacon Press.

Nun, José
1969 Latin America: The Hegemonic Crisis and the Military Coup. Institute of International Studies, University of California, Berkeley, Politics of Modernization Series, No. 7.

O'Donnell, Guillermo
  1973 Modernization and Bureaucratic-Authoritarianism: Studies
        in South American Politics. Institute of International
        Studies, University of California, Berkeley, Politics of
        Modernization Series, No. 9.

  1975 Reflexiones sobre las tendencias generales de cambio en el
        estado burocrático-autoritario. Buenos Aires: Centro
        de Estudios de Estado y Sociedad.

Organski, A.F.K.
  1965 The Stages of Political Development. New York: Knopf.

United Nations Economic Commission for Latin America (UNECLA)
  1966 The Process of Industrial Development in Latin America.
        E/CN.12/716/Rev. 1.

II. Sources by Country

A. Argentina

Altimir, Oscar, Horacio Santamaría, and Juan Sourrouille
  1966-67 Los instrumentos de la promoción industrial en la post-
        guerra. Desarrollo Económico 6(21, 22-23, 24, 25) and
        7(26, 27).

Cardoso, Fernando H.
  1974 Ideologías de la burguesía industrial en sociedades depen-
        dientes (Argentina y Brasil). Mexico: Siglo Veintiuno
        Editores.

Chu, David S.C.
  1972 The Great Depression and Industrialization in Latin Amer-
        ica: Response to Relative Price Incentives in Argentina
        and Colombia, 1930-45. Ph.D. dissertation, Yale University.

Corradi, Juan Eugenio
  1974 Argentina. In Latin America: The Struggle with Dependency
        and Beyond. Ronald H. Chilcote and Joel C. Edelstein, eds.
        Cambridge, Massachusetts: Schenkman Publishing.

Cortés Conde, Roberto
  1965 Problemas del crecimiento industrial. In Argentina:
        Sociedad de masas. Torcuato Di Tella, et al. Buenos
        Aires: EUDEBA.

Cúneo, Dardo
  1967 Compartamiento y crisis de la clase empresaria. Buenos
        Aires: Pleamar.

Di Tella, Guido and Manuel Zymelman
  1965 Etapas del desarrollo económico argentino. In Argentina:
        Sociedad de masas. Torcuato Di Tella, et al. Buenos
        Aires: EUDEBA.

A. Argentina (continued)

Di Tella, Torcuato S.
1962   Los procesos políticos y sociales de la industrialización.
       Desarrollo Económico 2(3):19-48.

Díaz Alejandro, Carlos F.
1970   Essays on the Economic History of the Argentina Republic.
       New Haven, Connecticut: Yale University Press.

1971   The Argentine State and Economic Growth: A Historical
       Review. In Government and Economic Development. Gustav
       Ranis, ed. New Haven, Connecticut: Yale University Press.

Dorfman, Adolfo
1970   Historia de la industria Argentina. Buenos Aires:
       Ediciones Solar.

Ferrer, Aldo
1967   The Argentine Economy. Berkeley: University of Califor-
       nia Press.

Fillol, Tomas Roberto
1961   Social Factors in Economic Development: The Argentine
       Case. Cambridge, Massachusetts: M.I.T. Press.

Freels, John William, Jr.
1968   Industrial Trade Associations in Argentine Politics.
       Ph.D. dissertation, University of California, Riverside.

Goldwert, Marvin
1972   Democracy, Militarism, and Nationalism in Argentina,
       1930-1966. Austin: University of Texas Press.

Jorge, Eduardo F.
1971   Industria y concentración económica: Desde principios
       de siglo hasta el peronismo. Buenos Aires: Siglo
       Veintiuno Editores.

Kenworthy, Eldon
1972   Did the "New Industrialists" Play a Significant Role in
       the Formation of Perón's Coalition, 1943-46? In New
       Perspectives on Modern Argentina. Alberto Ciria, et
       al. Bloomington: Latin American Studies Program, In-
       diana University.

Lindenboim, Javier
1976   El empresariado industrial argentino y sus organizaciones
       gremiales entre 1930 y 1946. Desarrollo Económico 16(62):
       163-201.

Mallon, Richard D.
1968   Exchange Policy--Argentina. In Development Policy--
       Theory and Practice. Gustav F. Papanek, ed. Cambridge,
       Massachusetts: Harvard University Press.

A. Argentina (continued)

Mallon, Richard D. in collaboration with Juan V. Sourrouille
1975   Economic Policymaking in a Conflict Situation: The
        Argentine Case. Cambridge, Massachusetts: Harvard
        University Press.

Murmis, Miguel and Juan Carlos Portantiero
1971   Estudios sobre los orígenes del peronismo. Buenos Aires:
        Siglo Veintiuno Editores.

Niosi, Jorge
1974   Los empresarios y el estado argentino, 1955-69. Buenos
        Aires: Siglo Veintiuno Editores.

Phelps, Vernon Lovell
1938   The International Economic Position of Argentina. Phila-
        delphia: University of Pennsylvania Press.

Polit, Gustavo
1968   The Argentine Industrialists. In Latin America: Reform
        or Revolution? James Petras and Maurice Zeitlin, eds.
        Greenwich, Connecticut: Fawcett Publications.

Salaberren, Raúl, Jorge S. Otamendi Groussae, and Rodolfo Martelli
1946   A Statement of the Laws of Argentina in Matters Affecting
        Business in Its Various Aspects and Activities. Washing-
        ton, D.C.: Inter-American Development Commission.

Salaberren, Raúl, Rodolfo G. Martelli, and Julio Fernandez Moujan
1951   A Statement of the Laws of Argentina in Matters Affecting
        Business. Washington, D.C.: Pan American Union, Division
        of Legal Affairs.

Schwartz, Hugh H.
1968   The Argentine Experience with Industrial Credit and Pro-
        tection Incentives, 1943-58. Yale Economic Essays 8(2):
        259-327.

Scobie, James R.
1971   Argentina: A City and a Nation. New York: Oxford Uni-
        versity Press.

Silverman, Bertram
1968-69 Labor Ideology and Economic Development in the Peronist
        Epoch. Studies in Comparative International Development
        4(11):243-58.

Toledo, Mariano
1977   Argentina: Nine Months of Military Government. Monthly
        Review 28(11):13-18.

Villanueva, Javier
1972   El origen de la industrialización argentina. Desarrollo
        Económico 12(47):451-76.

A. Argentina (continued)

Whitaker, Arthur P.
   1964   Argentina. Englewood Cliffs, New Jersey: Prentice-Hall.

Wythe, George
   1949   Industry in Latin America. New York: Columbia University
           Press.

Zalduendo, Eduardo A.
   1963   El empresario industrial en América Latina, 1. Argentina.
           United Nations Economic Commission for Latin America.
           E/CN.12/642/Add.1.

B. Brazil

Baer, Werner
   1965   Industrialization and Economic Development in Brazil.
           Homewood, Illinois: Richard D. Irwin, Inc.

Baer, Werner and Annibal V. Villela
   1973   Industrial Growth and Industrialization: Revisions in
           the Stages of Brazil's Economic Development. The Journal
           of Developing Areas 7(2):217-234.

Bergsman, Joel
   1970   Brazil: Industrialization and Trade Policies. London:
           Oxford University Press.

Bergsman, Joel and Pedro S. Malan
   1971   The Structure of Protection in Brazil. In The Structure
           of Protection in Developing Countries. Bela A. Balassa,
           ed. Baltimore: Johns Hopkins University Press.

Cardoso, Fernando H.
   1963   El empresario industrial en América Latina, 2. Brasil.
           United Nations Economic Commission for Latin America.
           E/CN.12/642/Add.2.

   1964   Empresário industrial e desenvolvimento economico no
           Brasil. São Paulo: Difusão Européia do Livro.

   1968   Empresarios industriales y desarrollo nacional en Brasil.
           Desarrollo Económico 8(29):31-60.

   1974   Ideologías de la burguesía industrial en sociedades
           dependientes (Argentina y Brasil). Mexico: Siglo
           Veintiuno Editores.

   1976   Associated-Dependent Development: Theoretical and Prac-
           tical Implications. In Authoritarian Brazil: Origins,
           Policies, and Future. Alfred Stepan, ed. New Haven,
           Connecticut: Yale University Press.

84

B. Brazil (continued)

Cardoso, Fernando H. and Enzo Faletto
  1973 Dependencia y desarrollo en América Latina. Mexico:
        Siglo Veintiuno Editores.

Dean, Warren
  1969 The Industrialization of São Paulo, 1880–1945. Austin:
        University of Texas Press.

Furtado, Celso
  1968 The Industrialization of Brazil. In Latin America and
        the Caribbean: A Handbook. Claudio Veliz, ed. New York:
        Praeger.

  1971 The Economic Growth of Brazil: A Survey from Colonial to
        Modern Times. Berkeley: University of California Press.

Gudin, Eugenio
  1969 The Chief Characteristics of the Postwar Economic Develop-
        ments of Brazil. In The Economy of Brazil. Howard S.
        Ellis, ed. Berkeley: University of California Press.

Harding, Timothy F.
  1973 The Political History of Organized Labor in Brazil. Ph.D.
        dissertation, Stanford University.

Ianni, Octavio
  1970 Crisis in Brazil. New York: Columbia University Press.

Leff, Nathaniel H.
  1967 Export Stagnation and Autarkic Development in Brazil,
        1947–1962. The Quarterly Journal of Economics 81(2):
        286–301.

  1968 Economic Policy-Making and Development in Brazil, 1947–
        1964. New York: John Wiley and Sons.

Luz, Nícia Vilela
  1961 A luta pela industrializacão do Brasil. São Paulo:
        Difusão Européia do Livro.

Martins, Luciano
  1968 Industrializacão burguesia nacional e desenvolvimento.
        Rio de Janeiro: Editora Saga.

Morley, Samuel A. and Gordon W. Smith
  1971 Import Substitution and Foreign Investment in Brazil.
        Oxford Economic Papers 23(1):120–35.

Schmitter, Philippe C.
  1971 Interest Conflict and Political Change in Brazil. Stan-
        ford, California: Stanford University Press.

United Nations Economic Commission for Latin America (UNECLA)
  1964 Fifteen Years of Economic Policy in Brazil. Economic
        Bulletin for Latin America 9:153–219.

B. Brazil (continued)

Wirth, John D.
1970 The Politics of Brazilian Development, 1930-1954. Stanford, California: Stanford University Press.

C. Chile

Arriagada, Genaro
1970 La oligarquia patronal chilena. Universidad Católica de Chile, Ediciones Nueva Universidad.

Ballesteros, Marto and Tom Davis
1963 The Growth of Output and Employment in Basic Sectors of the Chilean Economy, 1908-1957. Economic Development and Cultural Change 11 (no. 2, pt. 1):152-76.

Briones, Guillermo
1963 El empresario industrial en América Latina, 3. Chile. United Nations Economic Commission for Latin America E/CN.12/642/Add.3.

Burnett, Ben G.
1970 Political Groups in Chile: The Dialogue Between Order and Change. Austin: University of Texas Press.

Cavarozzi, Marcelo José
1975 The Government and the Industrial Bourgeoisie in Chile: 1938-1964. Ph.D. dissertation, University of California, Berkeley.

Davis, Tom
1963 Eight Decades of Inflation in Chile, 1879-1959: A Political Interpretation. Journal of Political Economy 71: 389-97.

Ellsworth, P.T.
1945 Chile: An Economy in Transition. New York: MacMillan Co.

Gil, Federico G.
1966 The Political System of Chile. Boston: Houghton Mifflin Co.

Inter-American Development Commission
1946 A Statement of the Laws of Chile in Matters Affecting Business in Its Various Aspects and Activities. Washington, D.C.

Jeanneret, Teresa
1971 The Structure of Protection in Chile. In The Structure of Protection in Developing Countries. Bela Balassa, ed. Baltimore: Johns Hopkins University Press.

Johnson, Dale L.
1967-68 Industrialization, Social Mobility, and Class Formation in Chile. Studies in Comparative International Development 3(7):127-51.

C. Chile (continued)

1968-69   The National and Progressive Bourgeoisie in Chile. Studies
           in Comparative International Development 4(4):63-86.

Johnson, John J.
    1965   Political Change in Latin America: The Emergence of the
            Middle Sectors. Stanford, California: Stanford Univer-
            sity Press.

Leiserson, Alcira
    1966   Notes on the Process of Industrialization in Argentina,
            Chile, and Peru. Institute of International Studies,
            University cf California, Berkeley, Politics of Moderni-
            zation Series, No. 3.

Mamalakis, Markos J.
    1965   Public Policy and Sectoral Development: A Case Study of
            Chile, 1940-58. In Essays on the Chilean Economy. Markos
            J. Mamalakis and Clark Reynolds. Homewood, Illinois:
            Irwin Publishers.

    1969b   An Analysis of the Financial and Investment Activities of
            the Chilean Development Corporation: 1939-1964. Journal
            of Development Studies 5(2):118-37.

Moran, Theodore H.
    1974   Multinational Corporations and the Politics of Dependence:
            Copper in Chile. Princeton, New Jersey: Princeton Uni-
            versity Press.

Muñoz, Oscar
    1971   Crecimiento industrial de Chile, 1914-1965. Universidad
            de Chile, Instituto de Economía y Planificación.

Nolf, Max
    1962   Industria manufacturera. In Geografía económica de Chile,
            Vol. III. Corporación de Fomento de la Producción, ed.
            Santiago, Chile.

Nunn, Frederick M.
    1970   Chilean Politics, 1920-1931: The Honorable Mission of
            the Armed Forces. Albuquerque: University of New Mexico
            Press.

Petras, James
    1972   Politics and Social Forces in Chilean Development.
            Berkeley: University of California Press.

Reynolds, Clark
    1965   Development Problems of an Export Economy: The Case of
            Chile and Copper. In Essays on the Chilean Economy.
            Markos J. Mamalakis and Clark Reynolds. Homewood, Illinois:
            Irwin Publishers.

C. Chile (continued)

Soza, Héctor
1968   The Industrialization of Chile. In Latin America and
        the Caribbean: A Handbook. Claudio Veliz, ed. New
        York: Praeger.

Stevenson, John Reese
1942   The Chilean Popular Front. Westport, Connecticut:
        Greenwood Press.

Strawbridge, George
1971   Ibañez and Alessandri: The Authoritarian Right and Demo-
        cratic Left in Twentieth Century Chile. Special Studies
        Series, Council on International Studies, State Univer-
        sity of New York at Buffalo.

United Nations Economic Commission for Latin America (UNECLA)
1967   The Industrial Development of Chile. E/CN.12/L.21.

Wallis, Victor Edward
1970   Foreign Investment and Chilean Politics. Ph.D. disser-
        tation, Columbia University.

Wythe, George
1949   Industry in Latin America. New York: Columbia Univer-
        sity Press.

D. Mexico

Alcazar, Marco Antonio
1970   Las agrupaciones patronales en México. México: El
        Colegio de México.

Anderson, Charles W.
1963   Bankers as Revolutionaries: Politics and Development
        Banking in Mexico. In The Political Economy of Mexico.
        William P. Glade and Charles W. Anderson. Madison:
        University of Wisconsin Press.

Anderson, Rodney D.
1974   Mexican Workers and the Politics of Revolution, 1906-
        1911. The Hispanic American Historical Review 54(1):
        94-113.

Aubey, Robert T.
1966   Nacional Financiera and Mexican Industry: A Study of
        the Financial Relationship Between the Government and
        the Private Sector of Mexico. Los Angeles: UCLA Latin
        American Center.

D. Mexico (continued)

Bernal-Molina, Julián
1948 A Statement of the Laws of Mexico in Matters Affecting
      Business in Its Various Aspects and Activities. Washing-
      ton, D.C.: Inter-American Development Commission.

1956 A Statement of the Laws of Mexico in Matters Affecting
      Business. 2nd ed. Washington, D.C.: Pan American Union,
      Central Legal Division, Department of Legal Affairs.

Blair, Calvin P.
1964 Nacional Financiera: Entrepreneurship in a Mixed Economy.
      In Public Policy and Private Enterprise in Mexico. Ray-
      mond Vernon, ed. Cambridge, Massachusetts: Harvard Uni-
      versity Press.

Brandenburg, Frank R.
1964 The Development of Latin American Private Enterprise.
      Washington, D.C.: National Planning Association.

Bueno, Gerardo
1971 The Structure of Protection in Mexico. In The Structure
      of Protection in Developing Countries. Bela Balassa, ed.
      Baltimore: Johns Hopkins University Press.

Cinta, Ricardo
1972 Burguesía nacional y desarrollo. In El perfil de México
      en 1980, Vol. 3. Jorge Martínez Ríos, et al. México:
      Siglo Veintiuno Editores.

Cockroft, James D.
1968 Intellectual Precursors of the Mexican Revolution, 1900-
      1913. Austin: University of Texas Press.

Cumberland, Charles C.
1952 Mexican Revolution, Genesis Under Madero. Austin: Uni-
      versity of Texas Press.

De la Peña, Moisés T.
1945 La industrialización de México y la política arancelaria.
      El Trimestre Económico 12(2):187-218.

Derossi, Flavia
1971 The Mexican Entrepreneur. Paris: Development Centre of
      the Organisation for Economic Co-operation and Development.

Germán Parra, Manuel
1967 Mexico Must and Will Industrialize. In The Meaning of the
      Mexican Revolution. Charles C. Cumberland, ed. Boston:
      D.C. Heath.

Glade, William P.
1955 The Role of Government Enterprise in the Economic Devel-
      opment of Underdeveloped Regions: Mexico, A Case Study.
      Ph.D. dissertation, The University of Texas.

D. Mexico (continued)

1963   Revolution and Economic Development: A Mexican Reprise. In The Political Economy of Mexico. William P. Glade and Charles W. Anderson. Madison: University of Wisconsin Press.

Goldsmith, Raymond W.
1966   The Financial Development of Mexico. Paris: Development Centre of the Organisation for Economic Co-operation and Development.

González Casanova, Pablo
1970   Democracy in Mexico. London: Oxford University Press.

Hamilton, Nora
1977   The State and Class Formation in Post-Revolutionary Mexico. Paper presented at joint national meeting of the Latin American Studies Association and the African Studies Association, Houston, Texas.

Hansen, Roger D.
1971   Mexican Economic Development: The Roots of Rapid Growth. National Planning Association, Studies in Development Progress, No. 2.

1974   The Politics of Mexican Development. Baltimore: Johns Hopkins University Press.

Hu-Dehart, Evelyn
1974   Development and Rural Rebellion: Pacification of the Yaquis in the Late Porfiriato. The Hispanic American Historical Review 54(1):72-93.

Izquierdo, Rafael
1964   Protectionism in Mexico. In Public Policy and Private Enterprise in Mexico. Raymond Vernon, ed. Cambridge, Massachusetts: Harvard University Press.

Katz, Friedrich
1974   Labor Conditions on Haciendas in Porfirian Mexico: Some Trends and Tendencies. The Hispanic American Historical Review 54(1):1-47.

Kaufman, Robert R.
1977   Mexico and Latin American Authoritarianism. In Authoritarianism in Mexico. José Luis Reyna and Richard S. Weinert, eds. Philadelphia: Institute for the Study of Human Issues.

King, Timothy
1970   Mexico: Industrialization and Trade Policies Since 1940. London: Oxford University Press.

D. Mexico (continued)

Labastida Martín del Campo, Julio
    1972   Los grupos dominantes frente a las alternativas de cambio.
          In El perfil de México en 1980, Vol. 3. Jorge Martínez
          Ríos, et al. Mexico: Siglo Veintiuno Editores.

LaCascia, Joseph S.
    1969   Capital Formation and Economic Development in Mexico.
          New York: Praeger.

Mosk, Sanford A.
    1950   Industrial Revolution in Mexico. Berkeley: University
          of California Press.

Reynolds, Clark
    1970   The Mexican Economy: Twentieth Century Structure and
          Growth. New Haven, Connecticut: Yale University Press.

Rosenzweig, Fernando
    1965   La industria. In Historia moderna de México, Vol. 7,
          Pt. 1, El Porfiriato, La vida económica. Daniel Cosío
          Villegas. México: Editorial Hermes.

Ross, Stanford G. and John B. Christensen
    1959   Tax Incentives for Industry in Mexico. Cambridge, Mass-
          achusetts: Law School of Harvard University.

Ross, Stanley R.
    1955   Francisco Madero: Apostle of Mexican Democracy. New
          York: Columbia University Press.

Ruiz, Ramón Eduardo
    1976   Labor and the Ambivalent Revolutionaries: Mexico, 1911-
          1923. Baltimore: Johns Hopkins University Press.

Shafer, Robert Jones
    1973   Mexican Business Organizations: History and Analysis.
          Syracuse, New York: Syracuse University Press.

Shelton, David H.
    1964   The Banking System: Money and the Goal of Growth. In
          Public Policy and Private Enterprise in Mexico. Raymond
          Vernon, ed. Cambridge, Massachusetts: Harvard Univer-
          sity Press.

Smith, Peter H.
    1973   La política dentro de la Revolución: El Congreso Con-
          stituyente de 1916-1917. Historia Mexicana 22(3):363-95.

Strassman, W. Paul
    1968   Technological Change and Economic Development: The Manu-
          facturing Experience of Mexico and Puerto Rico. Ithaca,
          New York: Cornell University Press.

D. Mexico (continued)

Vernon, Raymond
    1963   The Dilemma of Mexico's Development. Cambridge, Massachusetts: Harvard University Press.

Wythe, George
    1949   Industry in Latin America. New York: Columbia University Press.

E. Venezuela

Alexander, Robert J.
    1964   The Venezuelan Democratic Revolution: A Profile of the Regime of Rómulo Betancourt. New Brunswick, New Jersey: Rutgers University Press.

Blank, David Eugene
    1971   Political Conflict and Industrial Planning in Venezuela. In Venezuela: 1969--Analysis of Progress. Philip B. Taylor, Jr., ed. Washington, D.C.: School of Advanced International Studies, Johns Hopkins University.

    1973   Politics in Venezuela: A Country Study. Boston: Little Brown.

Carrillo Batalla, Tomás Enrique
    1962   El desarrollo del sector manufacturero industrial de la economía venezolana. Caracas: Universidad Central de Venezuela, Facultad de Economía.

Falcón Urbano, Miguel A.
    1969   Desarrollo e industrialización de Venezuela: Un enfoque metodológico. Caracas: Universidad Central de Venezuela, Facultad de Ciencias Económicas y Sociales.

Feinstein, Otto
    1965   The Role of Foreign Investment in the Development of Venezuela. Ph.D. dissertation, University of Chicago.

Gil, José Antonio
    1975   Entrepreneurs and Regime Consolidation. Caracas: Instituto de Estudios de Administración.

    1977   Entrepreneurs and Regime Consolidation. In Venezuela: The Democratic Experience. John D. Martz and David J. Myers, eds. New York: Praeger.

International Bank for Reconstruction and Development
    1961   The Economic Development of Venezuela. Baltimore: Johns Hopkins University Press.

Loreto, Luis and Rene Lepervanche Parparcen
    1949   A Statement of the Laws of Venezuela in Matters Affecting Business in Its Various Aspects and Activities. Washington, D.C.: Inter-American Development Commission.

E. Venezuela (continued)

Machado Gómez, Alfredo
1968   The Venezuelan Economic Structure and Its Changes in the
Last 25 Years. In Venezuela heute: Wirtschaftliche,
soziale, kulturelle und politische Aspekte. Latein-
amerikanisches Institut an der Hochschule St. Gallen fur
Wirtschafts- und Sozialwissenschaften. Zurich: Orell
Fussli Verlag.

Rangel, Domingo Alberto
1972   La oligarquía del dinero. Caracas: Editorial Fuentes.

Rollins, Charles E.
1955   Economic Development in Venezuela. Economic Development
and Cultural Change 4(1):82-93.

Tugwell, Franklin
1975a   Brief Report on Research Project on the Venezuelan Private Sector. Prepared for the Conference on the State
and Public Policy in Latin America, Buenos Aires, Argentina.

1975b   The Politics of Oil in Venezuela. Stanford, California:
Stanford University Press.